HALDANE'S BEST
COVER LETTERS FOR PROFESSIONALS

D1441693

Books in the Haldane's Best Series...

Haldane's Best Resumes For Professionals

Haldane's Best Cover Letters For Professionals

Haldane's Best Answers to Tough Interview Questions

HALDANE'S BEST
COVER LETTERS FOR PROFESSIONALS

Bernard Haldane Associates

IMPACT PUBLICATIONS
Manassas Park, Virginia

Library of Congress Cataloging-in-Publication Data

Haldane's best cover letters for professionals / Bernard Haldane
   Associates.
    p. cm.
Includes bibliographical references and index.
ISBN 1-57023-110-9 (alk. paper)
1. Cover letters. 2. Professional employees I. Bernard Haldane
   Associates. II. Title: Best cover letters for professionals.
HF5383.H18 1999
808'.06665—dc21   99-14868
                                  CIP

Publisher: For information on Impact Publications, including current and forthcoming publications, authors, press kits, bookstore, and submission requirements, visit Impact's Web site: *www.impactpublications.com*

Publicity/Rights: For information on publicity, author interviews, and subsidiary rights, contact the Public Relations and Marketing Department: Tel. 703/361-7300 or Fax 703/335-9486.

Sales/Distribution: Bookstore sales are handled through Impact's trade distributor: National Book Network, 15200 NBN Way, Blue Ridge Summit, PA 17214, Tel. 1-800-462-6420. All other sales and distribution inquiries should be directed to the publisher: Sales Department, IMPACT PUBLICATIONS, 9104-N Manassas Dr., Manassas Park, VA 20111-5211, Tel. 703/361-7300, Fax 703/335-9486, or *haldane@impactpublications.com*

Book design by Kristina Ackley

Contents

GLOSSARY OF LETTERS

PREFACE

Welcome to Bernard Haldane Associates. We're pleased you have decided to join us on what may well become an exciting journey, as well as a defining moment, in your career and your life—writing and distributing targeted, employer-centered letters that clearly communicate your career goals, major strengths, patterns of accomplishments, professional style, personality, and energy.

Like other books in the "Haldane's Best" series, this is not your typical job search book. ***Haldane's Best Cover Letters For Professionals*** represents the collective efforts of hundreds of career professionals who have successfully worked with more than 600,000 clients for over 50 years. Experienced in the day-to-day realities of finding jobs and changing careers, our work continues to represent the cutting edge of career counseling. Indeed, our innovative Career Strategy 2000 program, which interfaces with the Internet, provides our clients with quick access to today's new job search frontier.

Based on the career management principles of Dr. Bernard Haldane, the father of modern career counseling, this is much more than just another cover letter book filled with "do's" and "don'ts" and packed with examples of so-called winning cover letters. Consistent with Haldane's career management principles, this book takes you step-by-step through the building blocks that are so essential for creating powerful Haldane job search letters. Focusing on the "unique you," these principles will help you communicate your major strengths to the specific hiring needs of your audience. They also will help you develop important relationships that should expand your network of key contacts that are so important to your long-term career development. Employers should invite you to job interviews because your Haldane letter and resume speak their language loudly and clearly—they are looking for people who can add *value* to their operations. They want to hire your *pattern of accomplishments*.

This book is organized into two major parts. The first eight chapters outline the key principles, along with examples, for developing Haldane letters. They address numerous myths and mistakes as well as outline the different types of job search letters you should write during your job search campaign. Chapter 9 includes numerous examples of cover letters drawn from our client files. They incorporate the many principles outlined in the previous chapters. The names, addresses, and employers have been changed to maintain the confidentiality of our clients.

Bernard Haldane Associates consists of a network of more than 80 career management offices in the United States, Canada, and the United Kingdom (see Appendix, pages 144-149) that work with thousands of clients each day in conducting effective job searches based upon the many principles outlined in our "Haldane's Best" series of job search books.

So join us as we celebrate our more than 50 years of experience in helping professionals realize their career dreams. Whatever you do, make sure you navigate the job market with Haldane letters. Like Haldane resumes, these letters really stand out from the crowd because they speak directly to the needs of employers. They should guide your job search into new and exciting employment territory.

HALDANE'S BEST
COVER LETTERS FOR PROFESSIONALS

COVER LETTERS
IN YOUR JOB SEARCH

CAUTION: your job search may be endangered because you've neglected one of the most important elements in your job search—letters. Your cover letter, along with other types of job search letters, may be more important to landing a job interview and getting a job offer than your resume. Neglect your letters and you may effectively sabotage your job search.

Indeed, many employers report it was the unique quality of a candidate's cover letter that really caught their attention and resulted in an invitation to a face-to-face interview. After all, most resumes start looking the same after a while—lots of historical information about experience and education. But cover letters are different. Unlike resumes, they are perfect communication mediums for expressing numerous professional and personal qualities—professional writing skills, personality, enthusiasm, motivation, and direction. If you want to maximize the impact of your resume, make sure you write a powerful action-oriented Haldane letter, especially the classic, two-column "T" letter and Focus Piece (pages 32–39) that quickly screen many people "in" for job interviews. You'll also want to write several other types of Haldane job search letters that clearly communicate your goals, qualifications, and accomplishments to others.

THE ART OF WRITING RIGHT

Few people are really compelling writers who enjoy expressing themselves in the written word. For many job seekers, the written parts of the job search are laborious. Appearing to have no time to write, they prefer engaging in other types of job search activities—reviewing classified ads, exploring the Internet, or talking with people—than composing thoughtful letters. Other job seekers have no sense of what constitutes quality written communication—they send pro forma, boring letters and compose atrocious e-mail messages that are filled with spelling, punctuation, grammatical, and logical errors. They, in effect, kill their chances of getting an interview because they communicate the wrong messages: they are potentially illiterate, careless, and unprofessional—someone whose work the employer will constantly need to supervise. Employers definitely don't want such people interfacing with clients who would be aghast at such poor quality employees.

> *As a stranger to employers, you essentially are what you write. Make a writing error, and you may quickly kill your candidacy.*

The quality of your written communication says a lot about how the recipient perceives you. In other words, to the many strangers—employers—you initially encounter during your job search, you essentially are what you write. Employers initially screen you "in" or "out" of consideration based, in part, upon examples of your writing. Writing skills serve as a major indicator for eliminating candidates from consideration. Make a writing error, and you may quickly kill your candidacy. Employers really do remember the errors of candidates. And one of the major sets of errors employers report, relate to the poor quality of letters.

Whether you mail, fax, or e-mail letters, you simply must write right if you want to get that job interview and the job. When you write a letter, you send messages that go far beyond what you have to say in the written word. Like a Rorschach test, your letter says a great deal about your professionalism and your personality.

RESUMES AND LETTERS HAVE PURPOSE

A resume is basically an advertisement for a job interview. It's your calling card for opening the doors of employers who should be sufficiently motivated to call you for an interview. If you've written a resume according to the principles in our companion volume, ***Haldane's Best Resumes For Professionals***, you've already produced a first-class, future-oriented resume that should grab the attention of employers. Indeed, your resume speaks the language of employers. Rather than representing a compilation of work history, your resume stresses objectives, skills, accomplishments, and future performance. An employer instantly recognizes—usually within a 10 to 30 second visual scan—whether or not you are a "good fit" for the job.

But how did you introduce your resume to the employer? Did you send it by itself on the assumption the employer will know what to do with it? Did you include a handwritten note saying *"Here's my resume. Hope to hear from you?"* Or did you include a thoughtful targeted letter that introduced your resume to the reader?

We hope you chose the latter course of action by enclosing a cover letter with your resume. Furthermore, we hope you sent a well-focused letter that strengthened the content of your resume and motivated the reader to take action. That letter should refer to the resume, but it should not duplicate its contents. It should include a very special message that is consistent with the central purpose of your cover letter: motivate the reader to take action on your candidacy. Like a good advertisement, it should grab attention, deliver a powerful message, and result in action on the part of the reader. In fact, the principles of good letter writing are very similar to the four main principles developed for effective ad writers:

> *Like a good advertisement, your letter should grab attention, deliver a powerful message, and result in action.*

1. Command the reader's attention with an eye-catching headline.
2. Capture and sustain the reader's attention by presenting irresistible benefits of your product or service.
3. Expand credibility and desire for the product or service by presenting additional evidence, testimonials, and other explanations about the value of the product or service.
4. Stimulate action for purchasing the product or service.

As we will see later, your job search letters should incorporate most of these key advertising principles.

ASSUME READERS ARE TOO BUSY TO READ

Regardless of how well you present materials to others, it's safe to assume that most people are too busy to read and their attention spans are very short in today's busy sound-bite world. They read the first paragraph or page, skim or scan most remaining pages, and perhaps read the final page or paragraph. Materials presented in one- to two-page formats—executive summaries, synopses, condensed versions—will get the most attention. No wonder the *Reader's Digest* remains the most popular magazine (15 million circulation), and books with one- to three-page "stories," which make perfect companions for reading in waiting areas, such as the **Chicken Soup For the Soul** and the **Don't Sweat the Small Stuff** series, are today's recurring bestsellers. Most people either don't like to read, or they claim to be too busy to read. They need to be motivated to do something they ordinarily would not do, which is to read. Knowing this, you should be prepared to develop letters that motivate your audience to read both your letter and your accompanying resume. If you proceed on the naive assumption that your intended reader will actually read your materials in depth, you are in for some major disappointments. No one should be expected to read your letter and resume unless you make a special effort to motivate them to do so. You must give them *reasons* for wanting to invest their time reading your letter and resume. The major reason should be that you have something of extraordinary value—your skills, experience, and a pattern of accomplishments—that will benefit their operations, be it solving problems, saving money, or making more money.

That's our challenge to you in this book—write powerful letters that motivate the recipient to read and respond to both your letter and resume with an invitation to a job interview. You'll also need to write other types of job search letters that have similar motivational goals but with different outcomes—acquire information, schedule appointments, acknowledge assistance, or get a job offer. In the end, you should be able to write powerful advertising copy that will move the reader to make an expensive purchase of a unique product and service—you! For in the end, you should view yourself as someone who is marketing both a product and service that has great value—your particular mix of skills and projected future performance.

THE POWER OF COVER LETTERS

Many job seekers are surprised to learn how important a cover letter is to getting a job interview. They are even more shocked to learn about other powerful job search letters, especially the thank-you letter that often leads to a job offer. But many job seekers learn too late—after they've sent out numerous resumes with the same tired cover letter that goes something like this:

Please find enclosed a copy of my resume in response to your recent ad. I look forward to hearing from you.

Such a standard, wishful-thinking cover letter at best provides a cover attachment to the resume. It says nothing other than *"Here it is. Goodbye."*

And that's exactly what happens. Unless the resume is so exceptional to overcome this rather nondescript cover letter, it's *"Goodbye. I don't need to see you"* to this job seeker. The letter did nothing to motivate the reader to spend more than 10 to 30 seconds scanning the enclosed resume. The letter did nothing to motivate the reader to call the individual for a job interview. The letter did nothing to warrant even a perfunctory acknowledgment letter indicating the employer received the letter and would keep the resume on file for future reference. Worst of all, this cover letter diminished the potential effectiveness of the resume by not motivating the recipient to read it.

> *From beginning to end, your cover letter should clearly spell out why the employer should interview you.*

But this is exactly the type of cover letters most employers receive each day. They are nondescript letters. They accompany good, mediocre, and bad resumes. But they all have one thing in common—they don't grab the attention of the reader, which is the first principle of good advertising copy. Without some initial attention, your message, which is largely contained in your resume, most likely will be overlooked.

Like resumes, cover letters have the power to make the difference between being accepted or rejected for a job interview. They must be carefully crafted to go with your resume. Indeed, you should give your cover letter the same degree of attention you gave your resume since your cover letter should be an important linkage between you and the contents of your resume. In fact, you may want to dispense with sending a resume altogether and, instead, develop powerful Haldane "T" letters and Focus Pieces. These highly targeted letters tend to get read and responded to at a much higher rate than the standard resume and cover letter. Resume letters, which are used by some executive-level candidates and those who wish to broadcast their qualifications to hundreds of employers, also substitute for resumes.

TEST YOUR LETTER I.Q.

Just how well prepared are you to write some of the most important letters of your life—ones that could well change your career direction forever? Do your letters move employers to take action? Examine your letter writing and distribution I.Q. by responding to the statements on page 6.

Add the numbers you circled to the right of each statement in order to get a total cumulative score. If your total is 65 or more, you are well on your way to producing excellent job search letters. If your score is below

SCALE: 1 = very false 3 = uncertain 5 = very true 2 = false 4 = true					
1. I know what types of letters best move employers to take actions favorable to me.	1	2	3	4	5
2. I can write a unique cover letter that clearly spells out why an employer should invite me to a job interview.	1	2	3	4	5
3. I can write an effective "T" letter in response to a job announcement.	1	2	3	4	5
4. I can write a powerful Focus Piece after a referral interview and/or a job interview.	1	2	3	4	5
5. My letters always begin with an attention-grabbing first sentence or paragraph.	1	2	3	4	5
6. My cover letters always end with a clear statement of action I will take next.	1	2	3	4	5
7. I usually follow-up my letters by telephone within seven days.	1	2	3	4	5
8. My letters clearly communicate purpose, enthusiasm, and energy to the reader.	1	2	3	4	5
9. I thoroughly check my letters for spelling, punctuation, and grammatical errors.	1	2	3	4	5
10. I know when to send a thank-you letter.	1	2	3	4	5
11. I carefully craft e-mail messages with as much care as formal business letters.	1	2	3	4	5
12. I know when I should and should not fax or e-mail my letters.	1	2	3	4	5
13. I know the names and positions of the people who should receive my letters.	1	2	3	4	5
14. I have a clear strategy for distributing my letters to the right people.	1	2	3	4	5
15. I can develop an effective broadcast letter.	1	2	3	4	5
16. My letters represent my best professional effort and the "unique me."	1	2	3	4	5
TOTAL:					

55, you should benefit greatly from this book. In fact, once you finish this book, you should be able to score 75 points or higher on this letter I.Q. test.

THE HALDANE WAY

The Haldane approach to writing cover letters, as well as other types of job search letters, is consistent with the pioneering career management methods that have guided the job searches of more than 600,000 clients for more than 50 years. These principles begin with the notion that employers seek to hire your future rather than your past. As a candidate, you must clearly communicate to employers the "unique you" which consists of your pattern of motivated abilities and skills derived from an analysis of your successes

> ### Client Feedback
>
> *"I am ecstatic that I have received a position that is more meaningful than I had ever expected, and paying $200,000 in salary, much more than I expected . . . . I also learned that once I quit trying to do things my way and 'Just Do It' the Haldane way, that I began to make so many contacts that led me to this position."*
>
> —D.C.

or accomplishments. You develop a resume focused around an employer-centered objective that links your major skills to the employer's needs. Your cover letter should clearly spell out why the employer should interview you. It does this by showing how your skills and accomplishments "fit" so nicely with the job requirements. In addition, your letter communicates that you are a skilled, thoughtful, and likable professional who is prepared to add value to the employer's operations.

Join us as we share with you the many principles of letter writing, distribution, and follow-up that have proven effective for our many clients. These are important communication principles that can make the difference between being called for an interview or passed over for consideration. Regardless of how you distribute your written communication—mail, fax, or e-mail—the principles of good letter writing remain the same. In the job search, where you are constantly communicating your qualifications to strangers in writing, you essentially are what you write. Neglect your letter writing skills and you may effectively kill your chances of getting a job interview that leads to a job offer. Instead, write winning Haldane letters that really command the attention of employers who immediately say *"This looks like a perfect fit. Let's interview this person!"*

2

MYTHS, REALITIES, AND MISTAKES

Few people really know how to write effective letters. Many hold a set of beliefs that may be detrimental to conducting an effective job search. Rather
than learn lessons, they repeat the mistakes others make in today's job market. These can be costly mistakes that further delay finding the right job. Some
beliefs come from the advice of well-meaning friends. Other beliefs come from
logic that is not rooted in the realities of the job market nor in an understanding
of employers' needs.

Before you begin writing job search letters, make sure you examine some of
your beliefs about what does or doesn't work in a job search. What are the rules
and lessons you need to learn? You may discover some of your perceptions of
reality need to be altered in light of what we and others have learned about the
realities of the job search. In so doing, you should be able to develop a very
effective job search that focuses on what really works for job seekers—and for
you.

FOUR LETTER STAGES

Similar to a resume, your letters follow four distinct and progressive stages:
writing, production, distribution, and follow-up. Each stage has its own set of
rules for effectiveness. However, most examinations of job search letters primarily focus on the first stage, **letter writing**. This stage is preoccupied with crafting
the contents and developing the right language for a letter. It includes writing
different types of job search letters, organizing elements in the letter, choosing a
writing style, developing strategies for motivating the reader, and evaluating the

overall quality of the letter. The goal is to write a first-class letter that will grab the attention of readers and motivate them to take desired actions.

The second stage, **letter production**, focuses on how to best produce your letters for maximum impact. For example, should you handwrite or type (word process) your letters? What size, color, and quality of paper should you use? What particular layout and design seems to work best? Most production issues deal with how to make your letter look and feel professional.

The third stage, **letter distribution**, includes a host of important distribution questions. The main issue is how to get your first-class letter in the right hands where it will get read and responded to. Should you, for example, mail, fax, or e-mail your letter? If you mail it, what kind of envelope, stamp, and delivery service should you use? Should you always address your letter to a specific name or is it okay to send it to the anonymous "To Whom It May Concern"? And what about broadcasting a letter to hundreds of potential employers versus targeting customized letters to specific individuals?

The fourth stage, **letter follow-up**, is perhaps the most important stage of all. Unfortunately, most job seekers fail to follow-up their written communication. They assume the letter recipient will contact them if they are interested in doing so. But in reality, most letter recipients are too busy to read and reply. Therefore, it's incumbent upon you to take the initiative to see if the person has received your letter and has a response. The issues here center on proper follow-up methods to ensure a response. In many cases, such follow-up initiatives result in positive responses. Whatever you do, make sure you follow-up your written communication.

How well you handle all four of these stages will largely determine how effective you will be with your written communication and your job search. The following myths and realities relate to each of these stages. They reveal many of the key principles underlying the whole job search process.

YOUR JOB SEARCH

MYTH #1:   **The best qualified individual gets the job.**

REALITY: "Qualifications" can be a tricky term. It means different things to different people. Employers hire for all kinds of reasons. While employers want new employees to be technically competent to do the job, they also look for other indicators of success: focus, enthusiasm, energy, attitude, honesty, integrity, and social behavior—the ability to adjust to their organizational culture. Many of these personal characteristics or qualities will largely determine whether or not an employer will like you. In the end, "likability" will probably determine whether or not you will be hired. Indeed, studies show that subjective "likability" often outranks more objective indicators of qualifications, such as education, skills, and experience. All things being equal, the candidate that gets hired is the one the employer likes the most. That candidate is viewed as someone who can both do the job and work well with the boss and co-workers. He or she is a "good fit" for both the job and the organization. Consequently, you need to do more than just present your qualifications to employers. You need to present an all-encompassing "unique you" that goes beyond education, skills, and experience. While easier to communicate in face-to-face interviews, these other qualities can be expressed in letters and on resumes through the tone of your language and writing style. For example, does your writing sound like it represents someone who is enthusiastic, energetic, engaging, honest, and focused—someone who is very interesting both professionally and personally, a person the reader would like to interview and perhaps hire? If you can capture these qualities in your letters and resume, you should be well on your way to getting an interview and the chance for a job offer.

MYTH #2: **Most people learn from their mistakes. Knowing your weaknesses will help you redirect your career.**

REALITY: Knowing your mistakes and your weaknesses is interesting information that may help you avoid future errors. However, most people are better able to change their behavior and redirect their careers if they examine their strengths. If you study your successes—those things that are right about you and constitute the "unique you"—you will have a much clearer idea of where you should channel your career energies in the future. Knowing that you have a particular pattern of successes will help you redirect your career in the direction of greater successes. If you know your success pattern, you will most likely keep focused and motivated on what's really important to your future success. Best of all, you'll clearly communicate a sense of confidence and competence to others. Success tends to breed success.

MYTH #3: **The Internet is the key to getting a job. You should spend most of your time "surfing the Net" for job opportunities.**

REALITY: Internet job searching may be love at first sight, but only extremely introverted and naive job seekers will embrace the Internet to such an extent. Our advice: embrace the Internet, but don't fall in love with it! The Internet is a wonderful resource for conducting a job search. However, it is only one of many potentially fruitful avenues for getting a job. All job seekers are well advised to incorporate an Internet component into their job search. They also are cautioned not to go to extremes in devoting too much time on the Internet, time that may be best spent on more fruitful job search activities. While the Internet has the potential to increase one's job search effectiveness, it's also a deceptive double-edged sword: its bells and whistles can be extremely addictive, time-consuming, disorienting, and fruitless—a big electronic search and retrieval hole that can suck up valuable job search time. In fact, only a few job seekers at present get interviews based upon using the Internet. A well-balanced job search should integrate Internet job search activities with other important job search activities. Use the Internet to conduct research on employers, gather information and advice on conducting your job search, post your resume in online resume databases, survey job listings, and e-mail your resume in response to vacancies. But make sure you relate these online electronic activities to key off-line interpersonal job search activities: networking by telephone, conducting face-to-face referral interviews, and responding to print and/or word-of-mouth vacancies. Most jobs are still found off-line through nontraditional methods which have become the hallmark of the Haldane approach to career management. Our clients use the Internet, but they do so judiciously—only *after* they complete their assessment fundamentals, develop clear goals, and organize an integrated job search plan.

MYTH #4: **Individuals over 40 have difficulty finding jobs in today's youth-oriented job market. If you're over 50, you're in real trouble.**

REALITY: It's true that many employers prefer hiring younger workers, and for two good reasons—most are cheaper and more highly skilled in today's technologies than older workers. In other words, they represent better value to employers than older workers. Expect to encounter resistance from employers *if* you emphasize your age, *if* you lack current skills, and *if* your salary expectations are too high. Indeed, today's employers tend to equate the lack of current skills, high salary expectations, expensive health insurance premiums, and lack of drive and energy with age. Not surprisingly they are afraid of hiring individuals who both lack appropriate skills and expect to be paid more than individuals who have newer skills, who may work harder, and who cost much less. To hire such individuals, who invariably are older workers, means getting less value for your money. An employer would be paying top dollar for experience but would be getting less value in terms of skills and work output. But here's the dilemma: employers also want experience—the more the better. If you are over 40 or 50, you have advantages over younger individuals: lots of experience and a pattern of accomplishments which should be a good predictor of your future performance. You should emphasize these advantages as *strengths* you bring to the job.

You need to address possible *objections* that may be raised to your age. These objections usually come in three forms: lack of current skills, high salary expectations, and less energy and drive than younger employers. Under no circumstances should you emphasize your age alone as a strength because age, in and of itself, is not a positive. It's what comes with age—experience and proven productivity—that is viewed as a plus for employers. If your salary expectations are too high for employers, you may need to lower your expectations. Better still, be prepared to offer pay-for-performance options, such as bonuses and incentivized pay schemes, that should effectively neutralize objections to high salary expectations. While you can deal with many of these objections during the job interview, you should at least anticipate these objections to age at the initial resume screening stage. If, for example, your resume indicates you graduated from college 25 years ago, be sure to include recent education and training experiences that suggest that you are in a constant learning mode. Make sure your letter and resume communicate loudly and clearly that you (1) have current and appropriate skills, (2) approach your work with energy and drive, and (3) demonstrate a certain depth of experience that is evidenced in an attractive pattern of accomplishments that is likely to continue for a new employer. If you can do this, age should be no barrier to getting a job. Indeed, it may appear to be one of your greatest assets!

MYTH #5: **The resume is the key to getting a job.**

REALITY: There is nothing magical about a resume, or even a cover letter. A resume is extremely important to getting a *job interview* which hopefully leads to a job offer and a job. In fact, during the past five years, the resume has become even more important because of the role of the Internet, resume databases, and optical scanners in the job search. The problem for employers is how to better manage the resume intake process as well as screen the large number of resumes in order to identify a highly qualified pool of candidates from which to interview. A resume is a unique calling card for opening the doors of employers. Functioning like a mini-resume, the cover letter bridges the general purpose resume with specific jobs. While a resume is important to the job search, so is the cover letter and several other types of job search letters. But the job interview is the most critical to getting the job. How well you do in the job interview will determine whether or not you will be offered the job. The resume will open the door to the interview and may help structure the interview questions, but it does not get you a job.

MYTH #6: **The best way to get a job is to respond to classified ads, complete applications, send your resume to personnel offices, enter your resume into resume databases, and wait to be called.**

REALITY: Do you like standing in long lines? That's what you're doing when you focus on these highly formalized job search activities. Lots of people do get jobs using these methods, but these are not the most effective methods for getting a job. Most of them relate to mass application processes that attract hundreds and thousands of job seekers. The best way to get a job is to target specific jobs and employers through networking. The best jobs—high level and high paying—are not advertised nor recruited in the same manner as lower level and lower paying jobs. Your best job will most likely be found through word-of-mouth, a headhunter, sponsorship, or direct application. If you organize your job search toward jobs through these channels, your resume and letter distribution and follow-up activities will follow a different pattern from that of most job seekers who operate according to this myth. You'll custom-design your resumes and letters and use them as part of your networking activities for uncovering and targeting key employers as well as for contacting headhunters. You may even forego the use of a resume and, instead, use two types of effective Haldane letters: "T" letters and Focus Pieces. As for waiting to hear from employers, he who waits may wait forever. Waiting is simply not a good job search strategy. Effective job seekers follow-up at every stage of their job search. Tenacious yet professional, they make phone calls; they write thank-you letters; they send e-mail; they basically do whatever is appropriate to get a response from a potential employer. They assume employers are busy and thus do not feel obligated to respond to every job seeker. Therefore, it is incumbent upon the job seeker to follow-up.

MYTH #7: **Hiring a professional to help you with the job search is a waste of time and money. Anyone can do this on their own by reading self-help books and using the Internet.**

REALITY: Many people can benefit from using the career planning and job search services of a professional—if they know what they are doing and shop around for the services that best meet their needs. Most people, for example, need to do a skills assessment that is really the foundation for the whole job search. While such an assessment can be done on your own by completing a series of self-directed exercises, for many the assessment is best done with the assistance of a career professional who can both administer and interpret the appropriate tests. Moreover, many individuals can benefit from the structure and guidance provided by a professional. Those who waste their time and money on a professional most likely don't know how to best select or use a professional. Many hire the wrong person for the wrong purpose. Some even get involved in fraudulent operations. At the same time, some people can do the job search on their own with great success by following a few self-help books and using the Internet. But their numbers are limited. Whatever you do, don't be afraid to seek out a career professional for assistance. If you would like to consult a Haldane professional, please refer to the directory of Haldane Associates at the end of this book or visit our Web site for more information: *www.jobhunting.com*

Client Feedback

I can honestly say that Bernard Haldane Associates proved to be in a league of their own. With access to an extensive database of companies and an extremely educated, professional staff, there was a support structure beyond comparison."

—J.G.

LETTER WRITING

MYTH #8: **Job search letters are important but they are not nearly as important as other job search activities, especially writing resumes and networking.**

REALITY: If your letter is the first thing an employer sees, it will probably leave a lasting impression and thus have an important overall affect on your job search. Indeed, you may have only five seconds to make a first good impression with this letter. Expect the reader to draw certain conclusions about you and your competency based upon the quality of your letter. If, for example, you are skilled at marketing but you do a poor job of marketing yourself, what does that say about your marketing capabilities? If you say one of your outstanding characteristics is "attention to details" and then you make spelling and punctuation errors in your letter, what does that say about your professional competency? The reason your letter is so important to your overall job search is because it is largely responsible for making the first impression on an employer; it can make or break your candidacy. If you write a dynamite cover letter, you may be quickly ushered in the door for a job interview. Indeed, those who neglect their job search letters do so at their own peril!

> *Your letter is largely responsible for making the first impression on an employer; it can make or break your candidacy.*

MYTH #9: **It's not necessary to enclose a cover letter with your resume. Just handwrite a note on the top of your resume saying *"Here's my resume in response to your ad."***

REALITY: Never ever send a resume without an accompanying cover letter. To do so indicates your lack of interest and professionalism. You should always demonstrate your best professional effort when applying for jobs. That means carefully crafting a first-class cover letter designed to motivate the reader to read and respond to your resume. If written right according to our rules, your cover letter may be more important to getting the job interview than the accompanying resume.

MYTH #10: The only letter you need to write is a cover letter to accompany your resume.

REALITY: Cover letters are mandatory whenever you send a resume to someone. However, you also should be prepared to write several other types of letters which are critical to job search success: referral, approach, thank-you, acceptance, rejection, and withdrawal. Collectively known as "job search letters," they play a critical role in communicating your professionalism and "likability" to employers. Any of these letters could be the key to getting invited to a job interview or given a job offer.

MYTH #11: It's best to give your letters a "personal touch" by handwriting rather than typing your letters.

REALITY: This is really a dumb and misplaced idea. Handwritten letters are fine for sending personalized letters to relatives and friends. They also may be appropriate—although it's debatable—for real estate, insurance, and car salespeople who believe it's important to personalize their relationship with potential clients through handwritten notes. However, your new relationship with a potential employer has nothing to do with these types of relationships. Remember, you are developing an important new business relationship—your talent in exchange for the employer's salary and benefits. Always keep this relationship on a *professional level* by demonstrating your best professional effort. This means typing (word processing) your letters.

MYTH #12: The purpose of your cover letter is to introduce and summarize your resume.

REALITY: Like your resume, the purpose of your cover letter is to get a job interview. Indeed, you want to get as many job interviews as possible. For the more interviews you get, the higher the probability you will get job offers. Your letter should grab the reader's attention to read and respond to your resume. It's your written sales pitch—it tells the reader why you are the perfect "fit" for the job. Consider your letter the sales pitch and your resume the sizzle. This is your opportunity to emphasize qualities you may be unable to include in your resume—personality, professional style, enthusiasm, energy, focus, interest, integrity, and likability—but which are important precursors to being invited to a job interview. Your letter, in combination with your resume, should motivate the employer to call you for an interview. Your letter should not repeat what's in the resume. To do so would create an unnecessary and irritating level of redundancy for the reader. Take this opportunity to enhance your candidacy with information and a personal style that is not included on your resume.

MYTH #13: **The best cover letters are very short—a single paragraph consisting of two to three sentences is sufficient.**

REALITY: While a cover letter should be brief and to the point, it also should be effective. Use the space to move your reader to action rather than just present obligatory canned cover letter language. It should run no more than one page and include three distinct sections that correspond to an introduction, body, and closing. The first paragraph should clearly state your purpose—it establishes a linkage between you and the employer. The second paragraph should emphasize your objective, interests, and qualifications in direct reference to the employer's needs. It clearly states why the reader should be interested in seeing you in person. The third paragraph sets the stage for follow-up action.

MYTH #14: **Your letter should focus on what you want to do and what you have done in the past.**

REALITY: Your letter should be employer-centered rather than self-centered. The employer wants to know what *benefits* he will gain by interviewing and hiring you. Warm, personal, and professional, your letter should speak directly to the needs of the employer rather than focus on you. Minimize referring to yourself as "I," "me," or "my." Address the contents of your letter to "you," "your," "company," and "clients." Remember, employers want to know what it is you can do for them rather than sell you on what they can do for you.

MYTH #15: **End your letter with a nice closing that asks the individual to contact you: *"I look forward to hearing from you."***

REALITY: While this is a standard closing written to hundreds of employers each day, it's also one of the most ineffective ways to close your letter. If you want the reader to take action, you must close your letter with an action statement rather than a statement of wishful thinking. Begin with the sobering assumption that the employer may be too busy to contact you regardless of how outstanding you appear on paper. Therefore, it's incumbent upon you to take initiative to move the employer to invest more time in you. Be specific; let the reader know that you will be calling at a specific time. For example,

> I will call you Tuesday morning to answer any questions you may have and to arrange an interview if we deem it appropriate at this time.

MYTH #16: **The tone of your letter should be low-key and deferential.**

REALITY: The tone of your letter should be very professional. It must immediately communicate to the reader that you are a purposeful, intelligent, competent, and a likable individual. Your letter must not be too low-key nor demonstrate a beggar mentality. Neither should it be too aggressive, obnoxious, boastful, or pushy. It must demonstrate your best business communication skills. You need to achieve a certain professional balance that motivates the reader to really want to call you for an interview.

MYTH #17: **Proofread your letter once for errors.**

REALITY: While you should proofread your letter, don't trust yourself to catch all errors. As careful as you may think you are, chances are errors will get by you. You're too close to your letter to catch every error which can involve spelling, grammar, punctuation, form, organization, or choice of language. Ask two or three other people to read your letter. Ask them to check for errors as well as evaluate it for its overall impression. Does it really grab their attention and motivate them to want to meet you in person?

MYTH #18: **In your cover letter, let the employer know you are being considered by other employers. This will strengthen your candidacy—you're in demand with other employers.**

REALITY: Don't play hard-to-get. It doesn't work in most cases. Such a statement will most likely turn off an employer; you appear to be playing a game no one really wants to play with a stranger. If you want to impress an employer, do so by clearly communicating your interests, skills, and abilities in reference to the employer's needs. If you play the hard-to-get game, you will most likely find it's extremely hard to get a job.

MYTH #19: **You should include your salary requirements and references in your cover letter.**

REALITY: For most people, discussion of salary requirements and providing references should be left to the actual job interview. These subjects usually get discussed during a final set of interviews. You need to establish the value of the job as well as communicate your value to the employer *before* you discuss compensation. Nonetheless, there are two situations in which you may want to reveal your salary requirements prior to interviewing for a job. The first is when you are specifically requested to include your salary history or salary requirements in your cover letter. When you do this, try to specify a salary range rather than a specific amount: *"My recent compensation has been in the range of $75,000 to $90,000."* A range gives you room to reach common ground and negotiate, if indeed you are within the employer's range. The second case

> *You need to establish the value of the job as well as communicate your value to the employer before you discuss compensation.*

is when you want to be immediately screened in or out of consideration. You may not want to waste your time applying for a $40,000 a year job when you are really looking for something in the $75,000 to $90,000 range. In this case, insert near the end of your letter a statement similar to this one: *"I am seeking a position in the range of $75,000 to $90,000."* But it's usually best to state "open," "flexible," or "negotiable," or not mention salary at all in a letter. For as soon as you mention money, you show your hand and thus weaken your future negotiating position. You need to know more about the position and your expected responsibilities and work load before you can intelligently discuss salary. This usually occurs after two or more interviews.

MYTH #20: **Use your full name.**

REALITY: Only if it enhances you in the eyes of a potential employer. Your name is one of the first things a reader sees and remembers. It should not scream at the reader as being a potential negative. A stranger's name can have both bad and good connotations. If, for example, your official name is Jeffrey Conway Aristotle Bloomberg, III, consider doing a makeover of your name. It's too long and too formal. A stranger might think you are an odd ball of sorts— probably very formal, unfriendly, and egocentric. Indeed, anyone who would insist on using such a concoction of names probably is strange. In this example, the name Jeff Bloomberg would do just fine even though the official family name that appears on the birth certificate is Jeffrey Conway Aristotle Bloomberg, III. Academics and professionals often use their full first name and middle initial: Margaret S. Fuller or Richard L. Whitman. This is more formal and less friendly than Marg Fuller or Dick Whitman. When you sign your name, use your preferred name. For example, if you are Richard L. Whitman but are known as Dick to your friends, you might want to put a more friendly face to your letter by signing Dick Whitman above the typewritten Richard L. Whitman.

MYTH #21:   **Sign your name in black ink.**

REALITY: Blue ink is best because it contrasts nicely with black print. Avoid green, red, or other color inks.

MYTH #22:   **Enclose as much information on yourself as possible, such as transcripts, letters of recommendation, and samples of your work.**

REALITY: Less is more when communicating with employers. Keep focused on what's really important at this stage of your job search. Would you play poker with someone who believes stacking the deck is the only way to win? Such uninvited enclosures are a great way to depress your job search! Only enclose your resume with your letter. In some cases, the only enclosure will be your letter. It's presumptuous to enclose other materials. Indeed, they will make you look too eager, hungry, and manipulative. In the case of letters of recommendation, you will appear self-serving if you compile such letters and enclose them with your letter. After all, one would expect to have glowing letters of recommendation since the writers were asked to provide them. And if they don't glow, perhaps something is really wrong with the candidate. What other self-serving things can one expect from this candidate? Does he or she also get customers to write to his boss or write anonymous letters to affect important decisions? Such enclosures are a quick and easy way to kill your candidacy.

MYTH #23:   **It's better to have someone else write a letter on your behalf as your "sponsor."**

REALITY: Only if the person is well connected to or well respected by the person who has the power to hire. Sponsorship letters also are a great way to revive a faltering job search, especially if you're having difficulty connecting with the right people. Other "sponsors" may leave a negative impression—you're too lazy to do your own work! But these letters should be sent by the other individual and separately from your resume. A sponsorship letter is not a substitute for a cover letter.

Production

MYTH #24:   **It's not necessary to go to the expense of putting your letter and resume on matching stationery and envelopes.**

REALITY: Since you're supposed to be demonstrating your best professional effort, make sure your stationery match—letter, resume, and envelope. Don't be "pennywise but pound foolish" by cutting corners where it counts the most—first impressions. In the larger scheme of things, good quality matching stationery and envelopes are not very expensive—$20.00 will get you off in the right direction. However, if you send a resume and cover letter flat in a large envelope, they do not have to match.

MYTH #25:   **Use personalized, engraved stationery which best communicates a professional image.**

REALITY: You can overdo this image thing to the point of actually communicating a negative image—you're too expensive for our budget! In some professions, such as advertising, this type of stationery may be appropriate. But in most cases, producing your letter on good quality paper will suffice. Again, we don't know of any employers who have interviewed and hired someone based on the fact that they used engraved stationery.

MYTH #26:   **Type your letter but handwrite the address on the envelope.**

REALITY: Like the handwritten letter (Myth #11), a handwritten address on the envelope is inappropriate for this type of business communication. Again, you're trying to demonstrate your best professional effort rather than manipulate the reader psychologically with this worn "personalized" and "thoughtful" handwritten approach.

Most people are on to such tricks that are best left to real estate, insurance, and car salespeople. A handwritten address on the envelope will actually diminish the power of your letter.

MYTH #27: **Produce your letter on off-white or some other colored paper.**

REALITY: White paper really is nice, especially when it also is quality paper. It gives a very clean and crisp look to your message. In fact, too many letters and resumes are printed on boring off-white, ivory, or light gray paper. On the other hand, the color of your paper may not make much difference unless you are in some artistic or communication field where unusual colors are a plus—it demonstrates your unique creativity and attention to the colors of your profession. But we have yet to meet an employer who invited someone to an interview and offered them a job based upon the color of their paper! When in doubt, go for conservative colors which tend to hover around white. If you know your resume is likely to be electronically scanned, use white paper. Other colored papers may be difficult to scan.

MYTH #28: **Always print your letter and resume on heavy weight paper. Such papers communicate confidence.**

REALITY: The weight of your paper probably doesn't make much difference, except when it is excessively light or heavy. Any good quality 20 to 60 pound paper with high rag content will serve you well. These weight papers also are good for electronic scanners. Very heavy and coarse papers may leave the wrong impression—your personality also may be heavy and oppressive. Worse yet, they are difficult to electronically scan.

MYTH #29: **It's best to use stationery that is sized smaller or larger than your resume.**

REALITY: We don't know of any employers who have interviewed or hired candidates based on the size of their stationery! A slightly smaller size does stand out when covering the resume, but not enough to get an interview. Very small paper looks like the stationery used for personal letters and hence conveys a less professional image. Concentrate, instead, on refining the contents and language of your letter and resume.

DISTRIBUTION

MYTH #30: **If you don't know to whom to address your letter, send it to the Personnel or Human Resources Department or "To Whom It May Concern."**

REALITY: Always make a special effort to get a name of the person to whom you should send your letter. In most cases, this will not be someone in Personnel or Human Resources. The key hiring officials are usually found in departments or operating units. When you address your letter to a specific person, you have the name of someone with whom you can follow-up. Call the organization and ask for this information, including a direct phone number for following-up within the next seven days:

> Hi. This is Jim Burns. I need some information for a letter I'm sending to your company. Who's the head of your marketing department? What address should I use? Does she have a direct phone number?

Ask for the person who is at least one level—preferably two levels—above the position which you are interested in. If you have difficulty getting a name, or you are responding to a blind ad, address your letter to the CEO or to the nongender-specific title of "Dear Employer." Alternatively, leave the salutation off of the letter but address the envelope to the CEO. The fact that you bothered to get the name of a specific person for your letter indicates initiative. A letter addressed "To Whom It May Concern" indicates you didn't bother to do some simple homework. You'll also have difficulty following up with such an anonymous address.

MYTH #31: **Broadcast letters are a great way to expand your job search and get more interviews.**

REALITY: They are usually a waste of time and money—if you don't know what you're doing. A carefully crafted broadcast letter, which may run two-pages, tied to well-targeted mailing lists of employers and headhunters seeking your skills, can enhance your overall job search. It expands the scope of your job search by reaching potential employers you ordinarily would not reach through other means. However, the returns on such a direct-mail approach, which could be less than 1 percent, will probably disappoint you—for every 1,000 letters you send out, you may be lucky to get one interview. The keys to making this approach work are the quality of your broadcast letter, the mailing list, and timing. In the end, timing may be the most important factor: your broadcast letter arrives at the perfect time—when an employer is looking for someone with your qualifications.

MYTH #32:   **It's better to fax or e-mail your letter than to send it in the mail.**

REALITY: Only fax or e-mail a letter when requested to do so. Many employers still consider their fax lines and e-mail to be private channels of communication. The mail remains open to the public. However, more and more employers are requesting that letters and resumes be sent to them via fax or e-mail. Individuals conducting an international job search will heavily rely on faxes and e-mail to communicate with employers abroad.

MYTH #33:   **You should immediately respond to a job vacancy with a letter and resume.**

REALITY: Timing may be everything, but the old "early bird gets the worm" principle doesn't necessarily apply to the job search. In fact, the opposite may be true. Chances are all the early birds sent their letters and resumes at the same time and thereby inundated the employer with mail, faxes, and e-mail. As soon as a job is announced, wait three days before replying. By that time most of the other applicants have already responded and their materials have been quickly sorted into three piles: no, maybe, and yes. When your well crafted materials arrive a little later, they may get more attention and stand out from the crowd.

> *The old "early bird gets the worm" principle doesn't necessarily apply to the job search.*

MYTH #34:   **It's best to send your letter by an attention-getting next day service, such as Express Mail, Federal Express, UPS, or courier.**

REALITY: Unless timing is of the essence, it's not necessary to use such expensive services. Send your correspondence by first-class mail. A good alternative is the U.S. Postal Service's two-day Priority Mail which costs $3.20 for up to two pounds of material. Their red, white, and blue letter mailer does get one's attention. In many cases, your mail will be received in a mail room, separated from its envelope, and then screened by a secretary or a low level personnel specialist. Only the mailroom clerk may actually see your expensive attention-getting envelope!

MYTH #35: **Use machine imprinted postage rather than a stamp on the envelope.**

REALITY: This may not make any difference. The stamp may indicate you're using your own postage rather than your current bosses' postage machine. Again, only the mailroom clerk may see your envelope and speculate about the origin of your postage.

MYTH #36: **Send your letter and resume in a matching #10 business envelope.**

REALITY: The #10 business envelope is acceptable and most of our clients use them. However, you should consider using a flat 9" x 12" envelope, which may not match your stationery, if you're enclosing a resume with your letter. Flat letters and resumes are easier to handle than folded ones. Also, flat letters and resumes are easier to scan electronically.

FOLLOW-UP

MYTH #37: **Once I've sent my letter, there's not much I can do other than wait for a reply. If the employer is interested in me, he or she will reply. If I don't get a reply, it means they've passed over me.**

REALITY: Don't assume anything. Silence has lots of different meanings. A safe assumption—one around which you should organize specific follow-up activities—is that your letter recipient is probably too busy to reply to his or her mail. The failure to reply to your letter may be totally unrelated to the lack of interest in you. Also, assume an employer's level of interest in you can be increased if you take certain follow-up actions. The best type of follow-up action is a telephone call which may result in a screening interview for both you and the employer. You simply must follow-up if you expect to get a reply to your correspondence.

MYTH #38: **If you don't get a response to your letter within seven days, send another copy of your letter as a follow-up.**

REALITY: If you want to annoy an employer, go ahead and send another round of the same paper. Chances are the response will be the same—no response. The proper follow-up action is a telephone call. In your original letter, include a follow-up statement that prepares your reader for a telephone follow-up call:

> I'll call you on Thursday morning to answer any questions you may have concerning my qualifications.

Since this statement alerts the reader that you will be calling at a particular time, he or she should be prepared to handle your incoming phone call—either take it directly or alert a gatekeeper to respond to you. At least you should get a response which is better than no response had you not initiated this follow-up action.

MYTH #39: **The more letters you write, the higher the probability of getting a positive response.**

REALITY: Positive responses are largely a function of the (1) quality of your letters and (2) the frequency of your follow-up activities. Always keep good records of the how, where, and what of your correspondence, including copies of the original letters. These records should help drive your follow-up activities.

MYTH #40: **If you call to follow-up and get a human gatekeeper or voice mail, leave a message that reminds the individual that you're waiting for a reply to your correspondence.**

REALITY: Under no circumstances should you be so unprofessional as to leave such an inappropriate message. Your message should be very upbeat and brief. Say you are following up on your recent letter and leave your telephone number. Chances are you may need to call and leave messages five to seven times before your call is returned. Each time be very pleasant and leave a similar brief message. One friendly follow-up message that often works well is to indicate that you will call again:

> Hi. This is Mary Burton calling in reference to my letter of March 7th. My number is 777-281-4782. I'll be in the rest of the morning and after 2:30 this afternoon. If you don't have an opportunity to call me this morning, I'll call again after 2:30 today. Looking forward to speaking with you soon.

This statement alerts the individual that you are not about to go away through their continuing neglect. It often elicits an immediate return phone call.

MYTH #41: **Don't make more than three follow-up calls to the same person.**

REALITY: Make only three phone calls and you're about half way to getting a response. Many busy people need to be called five to ten times before they respond. You need to be pleasantly persistent with your follow-up calls. Don't give up until you've made at least eight calls. After the fifth call, shift to the *"I'll call you back again"* line in Myth #40. If that doesn't work by the eighth phone call, it's time to quit on the phone. Do a final follow-up with a letter, fax, or e-mail message. Move on to other employers.

MYTH #42: **Once you've been called for an interview, you're through writing letters.**

REALITY: You're never finished writing job search letters until you're on the job. One of the most important sets of letters you should write near the end of your job search are thank-you letters. After a job interview, for example, write a thank-you letter in which you thank the employer for the opportunity to interview for the job and indicate your continuing interest in the position. After accepting a job offer, send another thank-you letter expressing your appreciation for the confidence given to you and indicate your enthusiasm for joining the team.

23 MISTAKES YOU CAN'T AFFORD TO MAKE

Employers always look for reasons to eliminate you from consideration. Sometimes the signs are very obvious—there's no clear "fit" between you and the job since you clearly lack the right combination of experience and skills. At other times, the signs are more subtle yet just as telling—errors in presenting yourself in writing to the employer, from spelling errors to judgment errors, such as including letters of recommendation and addressing the letter to "Dear Sir."

For employers, there is no easier way to begin the elimination process than at the letter writing stage. Remember, with a letter, you have fewer than 30 seconds to make a good first impression. Your letters should always demonstrate your best professional effort and provide the reader with good reasons for wanting to interview and hire you. Your letters should communicate that you are an intelligent, competent, and likable individual who will bring certain benefits to the

> *With a letter, you have fewer than 30 seconds to make a good first impression.*

job; therefore, you should be interviewed. Above all, your letters must be error free at all four stages—writing, production, distribution, and follow-up. If your letter arrives with errors, chances are your candidacy literally will be dead upon arrival. Few employers want to interview someone who is careless in their written communication. The reason is simple: If this represents your best professional effort, then we don't want you coming here to make on-the-job errors that can be detrimental to our company.

Over the years, employers report numerous errors found on letters of job applicants. Some are careless errors whereas others are judgment errors. Many are what we call "dead on arrival" errors:

1. Unclear purpose or vague reason for writing the letter.

2. Fails to relate the needs of the letter recipient (skills and performance) to the strengths of the writer (skills and accomplishments).

3. Presents dull and boring contents—lacks sufficient energy and enthusiasm to motivate the reader to take action.

4. Looks very amateurish—unprofessional in form, structure, and design.

5. Includes spelling, grammatical, or punctuation errors.

6. Uses awkward language, including the passive voice.

7. Presents an image of an excessively aggressive, assertive, boastful, hyped, and obnoxious individual.

8. Focus and language are very self-centered rather than employer-centered.

9. Fails to reveal much about the writer's interests, skills, accomplishments, or what he or she expects to achieve in the future.

10. Lacks adequate contact information—only a mailing address.

11. Sent to the wrong person, addressed to the wrong gender, or mailed to the wrong place.

12. Misspells the recipient's and/or the company's name.

13. Reveals typing errors, including handwritten corrections and the use of correction fluids.

14. Too short or too long.

15. Produced on cheap copy paper.

16. Printed on an attention-getting colored or very heavy, coarse paper.

17. Developed as an obvious form letter addressed "To Whom It May Concern" or to "Dear Sir."

18. Ends letter with a wishful thinking follow-up phrase—"I look forward to hearing from you."

19. Fails to follow-up with a telephone call.

20. Handwrites letters rather than types them using a letter quality printer.

21. Uses inappropriate stationery and the wrong envelope size.

22. Arrives with the wrong postage—recipient gets to pay the overdue postage!

23. Fails to write several types of job search letters for different job search situations.

Make sure you write lots of different job search letters and that your letters arrive well and alive. They should become powerful communication tools that lead to job interviews which, in turn, result in job offers.

3

LETTERS YOU SHOULD
ALWAYS WRITE

The most obvious letter every job seeker needs to write is the cover letter—the letter that literally provides cover for your resume. Not surprisingly, this is the most frequently written job search letter, the staple of the job search business. These also are some of the most abused and controversial letters, with a long list of associated "do's" and "don'ts" experts regularly dispense to job seekers.

LETTERS EXPRESS VALUES

While cover letters are the most widely written job search letters, they are only one of many important job search letters you should be aware of and incorporate into your job search. In fact, many of these other letters may actually be more effective in getting interviews and job offers than the standard cover letter. These other letters, written in response to different steps in the job search process, help communicate similar values you attempt to express in a cover letter—that you are a focused, intelligent, competent, and likable professional. In addition, these other letters express one other important social value—you are a very *thoughtful* individual, someone who might make an attractive personal and professional asset for the company. If you forget to write these other types of job search letters, you will be neglecting some wonderful opportunities that lead to job interviews and offers.

Haldane letters are very focused letters. They are designed to move both you and the letter recipient to action that leads to job interviews and offers. If written, produced, and distributed according to our principles and strategies, your letters should result in interviews and job offers.

TARGET AND BROADCAST LETTERS

Most of our job search methods are designed to target specific employers who might be interested in your experience and qualifications. At Bernard Haldane Associates, we begin by assessing our clients' strengths (Success Factor Analysis) and then build a well targeted marketing plan based on those strengths. Using letters and resumes, as well as networking and referral interviews, our clients market their strengths to employers who are looking for a good "fit."

At the same time, we understand the unique dynamics of the job market and the often complicated process of hiring. Jobs don't just fall out of the sky for individuals who are highly qualified, who write terrific letters and resumes, and who spend countless hours networking for information, advice, and referrals and uncovering job leads. Connecting the right individual to the right job is often a function of *timing*. You must be in the right place at the right time to find the right job. Most individuals spend somewhere between 30 and 180 days looking for a job. During that period, only a certain number of jobs become available. The real challenge for job seekers is to discover the jobs that best fit them.

So how do you connect with the right job during a one to six month period? Our clients use both a targeted and broadcast approach. The **targeted approach** involves contacting employers directly through cold calls, referrals, and applications. They send letters and resumes to a variety of individuals who are part of an evolving network of potential job contacts. This is a labor intensive job search approach that involves the use of the mail, faxes, e-mail, telephone, the Internet, and face-to-face meetings. The focus of this approach is to develop quality contacts that eventually turn into job interviews and offers.

> ### Client Feedback
>
> *"I vividly recall our first meetings in March 1998. I came to you bitter and demoralized after several frustrating months of a fruitless job search. The feedback you provided was right on target; learning to know myself and my marketable skills helped me to regain my self-confidence and ability to once again successfully rejoin the work force."*
>
> —P.S.

The targeted job search approach is very effective. However, being labor intensive, this approach takes time. You're limited in the number of targeted contacts you can make in a single day. After all, there are only so many telephone calls you can make and meetings you can attend in a single day. You may, for example, be able to make ten new contacts each day. Projected over a three month period, this targeted approach may result in pursuing 600 contacts that turn into ten job interviews and three job offers. If you keep up this targeted job search pace, you eventually will connect with a job that's right for both you and the employer.

At the same time, you may want to accelerate your job search by expanding the number of contacts through a **broadcast approach**. This approach primarily involves broadcasting your letters and resumes to hundreds or perhaps thousands of employers and headhunters who might be interested in your qualifications. Your goal is to get your resumes and letters in as many relevant hands as possible in the hope that your timing may be right—someone may be looking for a candidate with your qualifications on the day your mail arrives. Furthermore, your resume and letter may get automatically entered into a database for future reference. The latest version of the traditional resume broadcast method is the commercial resume database. You get your resume scanned into such databases from which employers access candidates who meet their hiring criteria. An online commercial employment database, for example, may include over 100,000 resumes. The broadcast method is designed to quickly expand the scope of your job search. However, its effectiveness is questionable: for every 2,000 resumes you mail or e-mail, you may end up getting only one or two interviews. After all, this is a direct-mail approach that yields a very low return rate. The key variables for increasing effectiveness are the content of your resume and the quality of your mailing list. If you enter your resume into online databases, your chances of being contacted by employers who access these databases are probably very low.

We recommend incorporating both the targeted and broadcast approaches in your job search. While you should spend most of your time (90 percent) targeting employers within your expanding network of job contacts, consider including a broadcast element to expand the overall scope of your job search. Get an electronic version of your resume in as many appropriate databases as possible, but don't expect to get many results from doing so. Send a well crafted broadcast letter, rather than a broadcast resume, to at least 2,000 employers and headhunters. Again, don't expect to get many positive responses. However, if the timing of this broadcast approach is right, you may get lucky and be called for an interview that turns into a job offer.

These different job search approaches require different types of letters. The broadcast letter is a very special type of letter that substitutes for a resume. It follows a different set of rules from our other types of job search letters that are most relevant to a targeted job search.

COVER LETTERS: "T" LETTERS AND FOCUS PIECES

Cover letters accompany a specific enclosure or attachment. In the case of the job search, that enclosure or attachment is a resume and it tends to function as a formal application for a position. These letters may be written in response to two different "application" situations:

1. **An advertisement for a position.** Expect to encounter two types of ads. The first ad includes the name of the advertiser. It may also identify a mailing address (postal and/or e-mail) as well as a phone and fax number. The second type of ad is a blind ad which does not identify the name or address of the source. In this case, the advertiser could be an actual employer who wishes anonymity or a recruiter or employment firm that is collecting resumes and letters for its client. There may or may not be an actual job behind such an ad. The ads can be found in newspapers and trade publications or on the Internet, radio, television, and telephone job hotlines. In fact, more and more employers are using a variety of media, including radio and television, to announce vacancies. The most informative ads tend to be found on the Internet where employers can provide one to five pages of detailed information on a position and organization rather than confine their ad to the very limited "column inch thinking" of print ads.

2. **An inquiry about a possible opening.** In many cases, you may want to send your resume directly to an employer whom you think might be interested in your qualifications. Your goal is to get your resume in the employer's hands in the hope that a position may be available, or will soon open, for someone with your qualifications. If a position is not available, you hope the employer will keep your resume and letter on file for future reference. It may be scanned into an electronic database from which the company periodically searches for candidates that meet specific hiring criteria.

In most cases, your cover letter should advertise your resume. When responding to an advertisement, this letter should focus on how the requirements for the position best match your qualifications. Two of the most effective letters our clients write are what we call the "T" Letter and the "Focus Piece." These letters may or may not be accompanied by a resume since both types of letters can stand on their own as substitutes for resumes. The "T" Letter includes a "focus" section in which the candidate lists the requirements—using the exact wording in the ad—and then directly matches them to the writer's qualifications. The Focus Piece is accompanied by a cover letter that introduces the focus section which matches the requirements for the position with your skills and accomplishments. In this case, the focus piece may run from one to three pages. Both types of letters tell the recipient that you have *exactly* what they want and it gives examples to prove it (skills and accomplishments). You should only write these types of letters if indeed you have the qualifications as specified in the ad or identified by the letter recipient. For example, most ads will list minimum qualifications using this terminology:

- Must possess . . .
- Successful candidates will have . . .
- Requirements are . . .
- Minimums:
- Qualifications:

Your "T" Letter must address each of these minimums and give examples or supports for each. When structured as such, this becomes a powerful letter because it speaks the language of the employer. This is an impressive and thoughtful letter in which the candidate has literally "done his homework." Unlike the typical redundant cover letter that regurgitates what already appears on the resume, our "T" Letter goes that extra step in letting the employer know that you are completely qualified for this position. With such a letter, the reader need not second guess or interpret your qualifications. The focus section shouts loudly and clearly that you are well qualified:

Client Feedback

"The 'T' letter... helped me pull out the most important aspects of the position from the job ad. In addition, I received many great comments about my cover letters."

—R.W.

Your Requirements	My Qualifications
■ _____	■ _____
■ _____	■ _____
■ _____	■ _____
■ _____	■ _____
■ _____	■ _____

Take, for example, the letter on page 35 which comes from the files of one of our successful clients who responded to a newspaper ad. This is a classic Haldane "T" Letter that positions this candidate well in relationship to other candidates who will be sending a standard, and often sterile, cover letter. While in this case the "T" Letter is accompanied by a powerful Haldane resume, the letter could stand on its own without the resume. Together, the "T" Letter and resume are impressive enough to be moved into the employer's "yes" pile for an initial telephone screening interview.

"T" Letter: Responding to Classified Ad

16 Bella Vista Place
Cincinnati, OH 45206

April 16, ———————

Ms. Cecily Dorfmann
Vice President, Human Resources
Nadir Industries
257 Vine Street
Cincinnati, OH 45202

Re: Sales Manager, <u>Cincinnati Enquirer</u>, April 12

Dear Ms. Dorfmann:

As a Sales Manager, I have planned and scheduled direct sales programs and trade shows with consistently profitable results. Here is a list of my qualifications as they relate to your requirements for the position of Sales Manager:

<u>Your Requirements</u>	<u>My Qualifications</u>
2 years Direct Sales Management (Self-contained sales region)	Over 7 years aggressive direct sales management experience as proven by opening 8 area offices which escalated regional sales average to #1 position among 200 offices.
Individual Sales Experience	Dynamic individual sales success proven by exceeding all sales goals for 18 months and reaching "Top ½%" among 250.
Excellent Verbal and Written Communication Skills	Exceptional Communicator as demonstrated by over 40 major group presentations, writing "direct sales" promotional materials and column (reaching 11,000), and 3-day demonstrations at 22 national trade shows.
Problem Solving and Strategic Planning Skills	Excellent Problem Solver and Strategic Planner indicated by structuring daily control meetings for staff of 25 resolving problem of "peak time" business loss (increased 35%)
Marketing and Corporate Office	Strong Marketing Experience (4 years) at corporate office level, proven skills in creating innovative team format and realigning 35 inside-outside sales/support staff to generate 15% sales increase to $3.5MM.

Enclosed is a resume that lists other accomplishments that may be of interest.

I look forward to meeting with you to explore the use of my talents to support the growth of your company. I will call on Wednesday, April 21, to schedule an interview at your convenience.

Sincerely,

Susan Ariani

Susan Ariani
Enclosure

A Focus Piece is another variation of the "T" Letter. It is normally accompanied by a cover letter and does not include a resume. This Focus Piece is ideally suited for different job search situations: respond to an advertisement, follow-up to a referral or job interview, or accompany a thank-you letter. Here's an example of a cover letter accompanying a Focus Piece which appears on pages 37-39:

Cover Letter For A Focus Piece
(Also functions as a thank-you letter for a referral interview)

21 East State Street
Hartford, CT 03455

August 21, _____

Mr. John Marston
Vice President, Operations
ABC, Inc.
2441 Uptown Drive
Hartford, CT 03456

Dear Mr. Marston:

I wanted to thank you again for our meeting last Wednesday. I also wanted to express my appreciation to you for taking the additional time to define some of the areas where you feel my skills might have some impact.

It is of great value to me to be as clear as possible on what seemed to be most important to you. I also want to be confident in my own mind that my background, skills, and abilities, will meet these types of challenges, so I've taken the liberty of developing a focus piece for your review.

I clearly understand that there are no immediate openings in your organization, but I also understand the inevitability of change. As such, should there be an opportunity in the future where you might need help in these areas, I would like to know if you see me as a resource for this type of position.

To that end, I would very much appreciate your feedback, and will call you on Tuesday, May 6, to see what you think.

Thank you again for your help!

Sincerely,

Jonathan Edwards

Jonathan Edwards

enclosure

Focus Piece

Why Jonathan Edwards Would Be an Asset to Your Company

<u>YOUR NEEDS:</u>

GROW BUSINESS FOCUSING ON QUALITY AND BEING THE BEST, NOT NECESSARILY THE BIGGEST

<u>MY ABILITIES:</u>

"Volume growth of 37% doesn't happen without a lot of effort on your part. You are certainly aware of the importance of this project towards future growth with Roberts Cookies. <u>Thanks for your efforts!</u> It's great to see you accomplish a very tough goal. <u>Nice Job!</u>"
Jenny Aloe, Director of Marketing, Roberts Cookies

15 years in quality customer and account services marketing both intangible and tangible products based on:

Transaction successes:
• Secured competitor's accounts by accepting "Prove it" challenge resulting in exceeding competitor's 6 month's best in 6 weeks.

• Grew business 67% over previous year and secured three new accounts.

Long term relationship successes:
• Expanded product exposure by developing and implementing an advocacy program based on categorical research and customer trend studies. **Result:** Increased dollar volume 124% and additional item exposure by 145%.

• Selected to create and manage two test market programs simultaneously by developing marketing campaign strategy including sales plans and staff training. **Result:** Revitalized 3 year sales slump and increased market share from a 5th place position to a 2nd place position.

"QUALITY CUSTOMER SERVICE"

"<u>Great follow up.</u> It's really a pleasure to have a pro like you on the team."
Mark Burkett, Sales Manager, Star Bars

Developed a proven record of exemplary client retention and satisfaction through perceptive needs assessment, highly responsive services, and consistent follow through.

Provided clients with a more "user friendly" process by revamping support materials and documentation procedures resulting in 41% faster turn around

VERBAL/VERSATILE COMMUNICATOR

"...Handled his duties with outstanding professionalism."
William West, Manager, Rising Sun Grocery

Built a reputation for diplomatic, tactful, and need based business relationships.

Presented marketing plans on a regular basis to district, regional, and national management.

Facilitated numerous training sessions, both as seminars and workshops.

Turned around the company's #1 customer by listening to specific concerns. **Result:** improved relations and an additional 23% growth in sales.

Consistent, progressive recognition for strong, interpersonal skills through evaluations, awards, and reviews.

As a INTJ/Amiable Expressive, I am:

- Natural decision maker
- Builder of systems and applier of theoretical models
- No idea is too far fetched to be entertained
- Natural brainstormer, open to and seeking new concepts
- Keen eye for the consequences of the application of new ideas or positions
- Have a drive to completion, always with an eye to long-term consequences
- Difficulties are highly stimulating and love to respond to a challenge that requires creativity
- Communicates value and trust
- Natural tendency to be helpful to others
- Open, cooperative, and supportive
- Accepting, with a high priority to get along with others
- Achieves goals while establishing strong personal ties

"OWNERSHIP" OF COMPANY MISSION

"Jonathan's maturity, thoughtfulness, and good judgment have created a leadership record for him, engendering the respect of his reports, as well as other managers..."
Bernard T. Slaney, Future Was

Ownership to company mission recognized by 8 promotions in 7 years.

REFINED, EDUCATIONAL, "NON-AGGRESSIVE" APPROACH	"Jonathan, great job!! You're making a large contribution very fast!! Thanks for a great job!" Ezra June, Regional Sales Manager, Star Bars Extensive training in "Non-Threatening" techniques through: • Murray Associates (Sandler System - Teaches how to help the client find out what they need). • Wilson Learning (14 month course work including Needs Assessment, Social Styles, Creative Selling, Communications, and many others).
FAMILIARITY WITH BUSINESS CLIMATE AND KEY DECISION MAKERS IN HARTFORD	"...Well organized, thorough, dedicated..." Larry Cochran, National Sales Manager, Windjammer Communications Numerous contacts in the market, **but what is more important,** trained in and educated others in how to get in front of people by using referrals, cold contacts, etc. Have made over 5,040 market calls in the last seven years, of which over 40% were cold calls. Ability to get referrals from clients, co-workers, etc. Willingness and desire to network at chamber events, trade shows, etc. Read *Business First, Small Business News, Columbus CEO, National Employment News, Columbus Employment News,* and many others.
ABILITY TO WORK INDEPENDENTLY/SELF MOTIVATED	"Jonathan has many strengths, including being a motivated self starter along with the ability to complete projects thoroughly and accurately. He is always willing to take on additional responsibilities... and is very well organized, trustworthy, conscientious, and punctual." Larry Cochran, National Sales Manager, Windjammer Communications
SUCCESS	"I know of no other individual in my 10 years of management who has so consistently striven for and achieved success on a regular basis." W. Arlin Gossamer, President, Albatross Confections

Referral approach letters are some of the most important job search letters you will ever use. Indeed, for most of our clients, these are the single most important job search letters they write. The basis for an active networking campaign, these letters literally open the doors of individuals who can help connect you to others who may be employers or to individuals who know someone who might be interested in your qualifications. These letters can extend your job search network dramatically by linking you to many individuals who can assist you in finding the right job for you.

> *These letters literally open the doors of individuals who can help connect you to others who might be interested in your qualifications. They can dramatically expand the scope of your job search.*

The purpose of these approach letters is to get a Referral Interview. As we outline in some detail in our companion volume, *Haldane's Best Answers to Tough Interview Questions*, the purpose of the Referral Interview is to get information, advice, and referrals from individuals who are in the best position to do so. These letters must be tailored to each individual and situation. They follow a common four-part structure:

1. **The opening paragraph should begin with a warm, personal statement recognizing the person.** You should explain why you are writing to this particular individual. If you are writing because of a referral, make a personal connection such as this:

   > Mary Thompson, Vice President of MetaHealth Care Systems, spoke very highly of you and your innovative work in health care management. She recommended that I contact you about my interest in . . .

   If you are approaching someone without a referral (cold call), make the following type of connection:

   > I'm writing to you because of your experience in . . .

2. **The second paragraph should explain your current situation and what you are attempting to do.** Refer to your enclosed resume with special emphasis on better understanding your objective. For example, if you are seeking a position in health care administration, you might write:

   > I'm currently seeking a position in health care administration. The enclosed resume outlines my objective and supports it with some of my qualifications and achievements.

3. **The third paragraph should request a meeting to discuss your interests and goals.** Remember, since you are not asking for a job through this person, put the reader at ease by mentioning that you don't expect the person to know of a current opening. Your intention is to learn from this person. For example,

> Please understand, I do not expect you to have or know of any current openings. However, I would appreciate an opportunity to discuss your ideas, suggestions, comments, and reactions on how I might best achieve my objective.

4. **The final paragraph sets the stage for taking action on your request.** It alerts the letter recipient that you will be calling soon. For example,

> Knowing your time is valuable, I assure you I will keep our meeting brief. I will call you on Wednesday, July 23, to arrange an appointment.

These powerful letters can dramatically expand the scope of your job search. They help put you in contact with people who can give you valuable information, advice, and referrals. Best of all, unlike cover letters and broadcast letters, you will receive few rejections with such letters. Most people will grant you a referral interview and provide you with useful information for further refining your resume and connecting with others who can help you with your job search. After writing 100 to 200 of these letters and following up with the requested referral interviews, your job search network should expand considerably and be targeted on jobs and employers who are most interested in your qualifications and achievements. The example of a referral approach letter on page 42 outlines the elements of such a letter.

THANK-YOU LETTERS

Thank-you letters are some of the most important letters you should write during your job search as well as immediately following the acceptance of a position. Never underestimate the power of a simple "thank-you" expressed to anyone who assists you with your job search or who interviews you for a position. Indeed, employers frequently report the important role thank-you letters play in the hiring process. They are particularly impressed with candidates who express their thoughtfulness, indicate interest, and continue a dialogue through a thank-you letter. While not required, thank-you letters tend to give candidates an extra edge over those who only write cover letters.

Referral Approach Letter

8370 Sassafras Drive
Apt. 404
Richmond, VA 22102
July 11, _____

Mr. Thomas Woodward
Attorney-at-Law
P.O. Box 2141
Washington, DC 20013-2141

Dear Mr. Woodward:

In a recent conversation with John Dillon, Vice President, Management Information Services, General Data and Transmissions, Inc., he spoke highly of your experience in Systems Management and Project Implementation and suggested I talk with you.

I am looking for a new career opportunity and am seeking information. It is my intention to leave the life and health insurance industry and apply my skills in a different private sector business.

Please understand, Mr. Woodward, I do not expect you to have a job for me. It is my hope, however, that when we meet, you can provide information in the following areas:

- My professional presentation
- MIS requirements throughout the legal profession
- What size law firm would require someone with my experience and background

I realize your time is valuable. Therefore, I will call your office on July 17, to schedule a meeting at a mutually convenient time. At Mr. Dillon's suggestion, I am also enclosing a resume. Thank you.

Sincerely,

Jane Doe

Jane Doe

Enclosure

You should seriously consider writing thank-you letters in response to several different job search situations:

- After someone has given you their time or provided assistance with your job search, especially following a referral interview or providing a reference or letter of recommendation.

- Immediately following a job interview, regardless of how well you felt it went.

- After accepting a position.

- In response to being turned down for a position—the ultimate rejection.

- When submitting your resignation.

Not only is a thank-you letter a thoughtful action on your part, it also demonstrates your professionalism and helps continue a dialogue with the letter recipient. Individuals who write thoughtful thank-you letters also are *remembered*. And being remembered in a positive manner is one of the most important things you want to achieve during your job search. The more people who remember you in a positive manner, the more likely they will assist you in finding a position. Individuals who are remembered tend to get referred to others as well as called back for additional interviews and offered jobs. Like employers, many job seekers report that their thank-you letters were the single most important letters they wrote in getting a job. Their thank-you letters sufficiently impressed employers who remembered them as a competent, professional, and likable candidate—someone they wanted to join their team.

If you only write one thank-you letter during your job search, make sure it's the one immediately following a job interview. This letter can make the difference between being accepted or rejected for the job. It should follow these general rules:

1. Write a thank-you letter to each interviewer. In some cases, especially panel and round-robin interviews, you may be interviewing with five different individuals. Each of them will probably have input into the hiring decision.

2. Type or word process your thank-you letters. Remember, you're still operating in a professional business mode. This is not the time to demonstrate your personal handwriting skills, however beautiful they may be.

3. Keep your letter fresh by writing it on the same day as the interview, or at least within 24-hours following the interview.

4. Make your letter unique by being personal, specific, genuine, and energetic in your thanks. Avoid any hint of "canned" thank-you language that may

raise questions about your sincerity—is this another generic thank-you letter automatically written by another resume and letter software package?

5. Refer, in your letter, to some of the conversation you had with the interviewer to show you were listening with interest and enthusiasm. Especially stress the "fit" between your qualifications and the employer's needs as you now understand them.

6. Correct any significant misunderstanding you may have realized after the interview.

7. Confirm any follow-up action.

The thank-you letter on page 45 incorporates many of these letter writing elements.

Thank-you letters sent in response to other types of job search situations, such as responding to a rejection or accepting a position, can have a very positive impact on your future. Take, for example, the thank-you letters on

> ### Client Feedback
>
> *"I've learned just how significant a 'thank you' letter can be! ...I really do believe that the job opportunities that have been coming from 'out of nowhere' are, in part, the result of the 'thank you' letter. Haldane taught me that!"*
>
> —G.O.

pages 46–47 sent in **response to a rejection**. Can you turn what is ostensibly a negative into a positive, especially if you are very disappointed with the outcome of your interviews? Most people would not think of sending a thank-you letter in response to a rejection. After all, what is there to be thankful about? On the other hand, if you really wanted the job and were passed over, why not keep the door open by letting the employer know that you remain very interested in joining the organization? Perhaps another position will open up for someone with your qualifications, or maybe the employer soon discovers the person hired is not a good "fit"—you may be next in line for an offer! Furthermore, in response to your unusual thank-you letter, the employer may go out of his or her way to refer you to another employer who might be very interested in your qualifications.

> *The rejection thank-you letter will most likely be remembered by the employer who may contact you for another position or refer you to someone else.*

If you've interviewed for a position and were not selected, send a nice thank-you letter in which you express your appreciation for the opportunity to interview for the position, indicate your disappointment in not being selected, and mention your continuing interest in the organization. This type of thank-you letter will most likely be remembered by the employer who may contact you for another position or refer you to someone else. The point here, as well as with most thank-you letters, is that your goal should be to continue

Thank-You Letter: Following an Interview

2800 Grace Avenue
Denver, CO 85208

November 3, _____

Ms. Elizabeth Galway
New Project Manager
Horizon Inc.
701 West Fourth Street
Denver, CO 85202

Dear Ms. Galway:

Thank you for our meeting on Thursday, October 30. Since that time I have had time to think over what you told me about Horizon Inc. I am excited by what I heard and I think Horizon Inc. is the sort of firm where I could make a real contribution.

My extensive project management background could be useful in "208" work and in developing plans under new provisions of the Land and Water Conservation Fund and Coastal Zone Management Act.

I am enthusiastic about the work near Cairo which was mentioned in passing. I would like to know more about it.

May I have an opportunity to sit down with you to discuss, briefly, these and related areas where I can make specific contributions? I will call you on Thursday, October 22, to set up a meeting at a time of your convenience.

Sincerely,

J. Richard Cunningham

J. Richard Cunningham

Note: If a second appointment has already been scheduled, use this letter as a thank-you and confirmation of a second interview.

Thank-You Letter: Responding to a Rejection
(Keep doors open)

2432 Wilson Boulevard
Milwaukee, WI 55555

September 23, _____

Mr. Larry Spartis
e-Management Associates
7231 Highside Way, Suite 302
Milwaukee, WI 55554

Dear Mr. Spartis:

I appreciated the opportunity to interview for the Director of Research position with your company. While I'm disappointed in not being selected for this position, I do want you to know of my continuing interest in your company.

The interviews were conducted in a very professional manner, I learned a great deal, and I enjoyed meeting with you and your very talented and enthusiastic staff. E-Management Associates is exactly the type of exciting organization I'm interested in working with and building a career.

Please keep me in mind if and when another position becomes available for someone with my qualifications. Best wishes to you and your staff.

Sincerely,

Mary P. Wheeler

Mary P. Wheeler

Thank-You Letter: Responding to a Rejection
(Focus on alternative position)

3731 High Street
Madison, NJ 02222

November 7, _____

Gerald Stevens, President
Tyco Textiles Group
24 W. 24th Street, Suite 207
Pittsburgh, PA 17777

Dear Mr. Stevens:

Congratulations on filling the position of Vice President of Marketing. Having known
Rachel Walsh for over ten years, I've been very impressed with her energy and
accomplishments, especially when she was Director of Asian Markets in Hong Kong. I'm
sure you'll be pleased with her work. She's also a terrific person!

While I'm disappointed in not being selected, I would appreciate being considered for the
new position we discussed during the interview—Director of Asia and Pacific Markets.
You mentioned the possibility of creating this position within the next few weeks. As I
indicated on my resume and during the interview, my five years of overseas experience in
Hong Kong, Singapore, and Australia are ideally suited for this position. During that time, I
increased MG Textile's market share throughout Asia and the Pacific by more than
500%. Indeed, I believe this position would be a perfect fit for both of us.

Please keep me in mind as you recruit for other positions. I'm very impressed with Tyco
Textile Group. It's the type of organization I would like to work with in the future.

Sincerely,

Daniel Ackers

Daniel Ackers

to build your network and turn negative situations into new opportunities. In so doing, your thank-you letter may:

- keep the door open with the employer who then considers you for another position
- result in being referred to others who can either assist you with your job search or interview you for a position

You also should send a thank-you letter to an employer with whom you are **accepting a position**, similar to the one on page 49. One of the major reasons for doing this is to get your relationship off on a very positive note. Even though you have been hired, you're still an unknown quantity with the employer. One of the employer's major concerns during the first 90 days will be whether or not you were a good hiring decision. You looked good on paper, you did well in the interview, and you passed the reference check. Now it's time you performed for this employer who has high hopes of having made the right hiring decision. When you send a thank-you letter expressing your appreciation for the employer's confidence in you and reaffirming your commitment to the organization, this letter becomes your first post-hire action with the employer. You have now begun building a positive on-the-job relationship with the employer. Indeed, this letter will most likely set an important tone for your relationship—you are a very thoughtful professional who the employer will *like* working with. How well you connected during the interview and the first few actions you've taken with the employer may well determine your future relationship with the employer. Your letter should be your first positive launch into this new organization.

If you decide to turn down a job offer, be sure to send a nice **declining an offer thank-you letter**, like the example on page 50. After all, individuals in this company invested time in your candidacy and judged you as someone who would bring value to their organization and with whom they wanted to build a relationship. These same people may play an important role in your future, either as potential clients or as an employer. Let them know you appreciated their confidence in you. Include them in your on-going network of professional contacts. As you've probably already discovered, it's a "small world" in many professional circles.

And don't forget to send a nice **thank-you resignation letter**, similar to the ones on pages 51–52, to your current employer, even if you are leaving on less than friendly terms. In most situations, you need to give a minimum of two-weeks notice that you are leaving. In your letter of resignation, recall the positive aspects of your relationship. Express your thanks for the opportunity to work with the employer, mention a few of your contributions, and end by keeping your doors open for a continuing professional relationship. This is not the time to settle old

Thank-You Letter: Accepting a Position

College Station
Box 265
Williamsburg, VA 23186

May 10, _____

Mr. John L. Harris
Management Recruiter
The A.B.C. Company
2835 King Street
Baltimore, MD 30715

Dear Mr. Harris:

I am writing to confirm our telephone conversation in which I accepted with pleasure your offer of a systems analyst position as outlined in your letter of May 1, 1999. As we agreed, I will plan to report to your office at 8:00 a.m. on June 1st. I understand my employment is contingent upon a satisfactory security clearance and negative results on a drug test that will be administered on my first day of work.

I look forward to a challenging and rewarding career with the A.B.C. Company. Your personal interest and assistance in my employment is greatly appreciated.

Sincerely yours,

Mary L. Doe

Mary L. Doe

Thank-You Letter: Declining a Job Offer

College Station
Box 265
Williamsburg, VA 23186

May 10, _____

Mr. John L. Harris
Management Recruiter
The A.B.C. Company
2835 King Street
Baltimore, MD 30715

Dear Mr. Harris:

After considerable thought, I have decided not to accept your offer of employment as outlined in your letter of May 1, ____. In view of my pleasant contacts with you and others at The A.B.C. Company, this has been a very difficult decision. However, I feel I have made the correct decision for this point in my career.

Thank you for your time, effort and consideration. Your confidence in me is sincerely appreciated and I will always hold The A.B.C. Company in high regard.

Sincerely yours,

Mary L. Doe

Mary L. Doe

Thank-You Letter: Resigning From a Position
(Leaving to further education)

223 W. Front Street
Tucson, AZ 88888

July 8, ————

Daryl Hinsdale
MJ Plastics Company
281 Silversmith Park
Tucson, AZ 88889

Dear Ms. Hinsdale:

When I joined MJ Plastics five years ago, I did so with the expectation of staying with the company for at least three years. I've learned a great deal and have enjoyed working with you. However, I've also learned there is a season for everything, especially when it comes to one's education and career.

After serious consideration, I've decided to pursue my MBA at the University of Arizona with special emphasis on International Marketing and Production Management. Since this is a very rigorous program, it's best that I pursue this degree on a full-time basis. Therefore, I will be resigning my position with MJ Plastics effective August 8, or sooner if you so desire. I wanted to give you more than the customary two weeks notice.

I've thoroughly enjoyed working with you, and I've really appreciated your encouragement and support. We've done some exciting projects together. I know I'll miss working with you. It has been a very positive experience both personally and professionally. While I will be a full-time student during the next 18 months, I will be available for part-time consultation. Please let me know if I can be of any assistance.

Best wishes.

Sincerely,

John Stellar

John Stellar

Thank-You Letter: Resigning From a Position
(Leaving for another position and company)

4721 Gillian Place
Detroit, MI 45555

March 12, _____

Harriett Marshall, Director
Human Resources Department
Glostar Department Store
123 Ford Avenue
Detroit, MI 45588

Dear Harriett:

I've really enjoyed my five years with Glostar, and especially working with you as your assistant during the past three years. You've been a wonderful mentor. I've learned a great deal and have grown considerably in my position.

But it's time I moved on to another position and company. I've accepted the position of Director of Human Resources with Tri-Mac Computer Company in Minneapolis. Formed in 1994, it's a relatively new company that now employs over 3,000 in seven different states. This is an exciting opportunity for me and my family. I'm sure we'll have a chance to meet in our usual professional circles, especially at the annual SHRM conference which will be held in Minneapolis in June.

I've informed my new employer that my last day with Glostar will be March 27, two weeks from today. They want me to report to work on April 1.

Again, I want to thank you for all your support and encouragement. I'll miss working with you and our staff as well as completing our new Internet recruitment project. Please let me know what we need to do to make sure this transition goes as smoothly as possible. And let's keep in touch!

Sincerely,

Steve McAdams

Steve McAdams

scores or to express any negative feelings about your job or the employer. What would be the point of doing so? As a professional, you should be bigger than that. This is a good time to mend any fences. You want your previous employer to remember you in a positive light and perhaps play an important role in your network. After all, you may well meet again in some other professional roles. And who knows, you may even be doing business with each other soon or end up working again with this person in a few years! Professional worlds often tend to be small worlds where your past has an uncanny way of repeating itself.

The point of these thank-you letters is to develop, maintain, and further build positive relationships with employers. You are networking, and it's the unique quality of your network that is critically important to your current job search as well as your future professional development.

The examples of thank-you letters on pages 45–52 further illustrate the principles outlined here. A good rule of thumb to follow is this: always send a thank-you letter regardless of the outcome of your situation. Thank-you letters give you an opportunity to once again communicate your uniqueness to employers, develop relationships, and be remembered and referred. In many respects, they are the lifeblood of any job search that is often characterized by numerous rejections. Thank-you letters have the potential of turning negatives into positives and thereby increasing your number of referrals and acceptances. In the end, the most important job search letters you write may well be thank-you letters.

> *Always send a thank-you letter regardless of the outcome of your situation.*

FOLLOW-UP LETTERS

The critical missing link in many job searches is follow-up. Many job seekers send resumes and letters but they never follow-up. They assume the letter recipient will take the initiative to contact them. If not, they probably aren't interested in their candidacy. In reality, many employers do not respond because they are too busy or they may have overlooked your resume and letter. Whatever the case, it's in your interest to follow-up on *all* important job leads and applications.

If you're spending time and money to initiate a contact, be sure you follow-up. The act of following up can make the difference between being accepted or rejected for an interview. Following up indicates that you are organized, interested, and take initiative—important qualities sought by many employers. Most important of all, following up means you will get a response. If it's a positive response, then you are off to the next stage of your job search—an interview. If it's a negative response, then you need not worry any longer or spend more time with this contact. Either way, acceptance or rejection, your job search keeps moving along.

And that's precisely what you want to do—keep your job search moving into more and more fruitful directions.

We prefer doing follow ups by phone and in reference to a specific follow-up statement near the end of a cover letter stating that you will be calling on a particular day to schedule an interview. However, after making eight phone calls and leaving eight messages with gatekeepers and voice mail programs, it's probably time to write a follow-up letter and move on. Don't prematurely stop making follow-up telephone calls after only three or four tries. You will often get a response after five to eight follow-up calls. But after eight unanswered telephone messages, it's time to write a follow-up letter and move on to more productive activities. This follow-up letter may result in a response. Some candidates have had luck in getting a written response by enclosing a self-addressed stamped postcard that includes three alternative checklist items:

> *Don't prematurely stop making phone calls after only three or four tries.*

- We're still in the process of selecting candidates. We expect to make a decision by _____.

- We've already made our decision and you were not selected.

- We would like to interview you on _____. Call _____ at _____ to schedule an appointment.

The examples of follow-up letters on pages 56 and 57 are used to get action and influence decision-making. The first letter on page 56, written as a follow-up to a job interview, is very assertive; it substitutes for a self-addressed, stamped postcard that gives the employer three response options. A similar follow-up letter could be written as an inquiry concerning the status of your resume or application.

The second follow-up letter on page 57 provides additional information to help the letter recipient make a decision following a job interview or it adds more information about one's qualifications which the letter recipient may already have. This letter also could function as a supplement to a resume or another type of letter.

SPECIAL LETTERS

There may be other occasions during your job search that require special types of letters. For example, you may need to write letters:

- requesting that someone write a letter of recommendation (page 58)
- asking for information about a particular company (page 59)

- seeking additional information about a position (page 60)
- clarifying questions raised during an interview (page 61)
- withdrawing yourself from consideration for a particular position (page 62)
- announcing the fact that you have accepted a position elsewhere (page 63)

Whatever the occasion for writing these various letters, be sure you put forward your best professional effort. Throughout your job search—as well as immediately in the aftermath of accepting a position—you are on stage demonstrating that you are a focused, intelligent, competent, and likable professional. Make sure all of your letters express these values. They should reflect your very best effort at communicating your "fitness" to others. For in the end, you are what you write—at least to the many strangers who must make quick judgments about you based upon your writing skills.

Assertive "Request For Status" Follow-Up Letter
(Used when interest was generated to some degree during a job
interview, but contact has not been reestablished)

21 East State Street
Columbus, OH 43215

August 6, _____

Mr. Thomas Rogers
Operations Director
ABC, Inc.
32 Jones Avenue
Columbus, OH 43280

Dear Mr. Rogers:

I want to thank you again for the meeting we had three weeks ago. I wanted to also restate my strong interest in continuing discussions to determine how my skills and talents can assist you with the challenges you're experiencing in getting ISO certified.

As you know, I have tried to contact you several times in the last few days, but have been unable to get directly through to you. While I am aware that changes do occur which alter situations and plans, I am very interested in knowing where we are in this discussion.

In that regard, I would appreciate greatly if you could provide some feedback so I will know what to expect. If:

1. I need to wait and be patient; I can do that!
2. I need to provide more information or take some initiative; I will do that!
3. I need to continue my marketing campaign to find another position because you are no longer interested in me as a resource; I would like to know that!

Once again, I'm very interested in continuing our discussions, but would appreciate knowing one way or the other. Thank you in advance for your call to (614) 999-8888 with this status.

Sincerely,

John Hartwell

John Hartwell

Follow-Up Piece
(For after first job interview, network update, supplement)

WHAT HAVE...

Julie Sanchez, President/Owner, MBD Brokerage
Jeff Williams, V. P. of Sales, National Sprocket Associates
Bill Crawford, National Sales Manager, Upper Limits Co., Inc.
Nancy Brighter, V. P. of Sales/Marketing, Borden Communications, Inc.
Kelly Haughter, National Sales Manager, Borden Communications, Inc.
Mac Dodson, Sales Director, Telecom Limited
&
Andrew Lipinsky, Regional Sales Manager, Circle Snack Co.

...SAID ABOUT MY ABILITIES

- "Volume growth of +37% doesn't happen without a lot of effort on David Jones' part. You are certainly aware of the importance of this project towards future (company) growth with M&M Mars. **Thanks for your** efforts! It's great to see you accomplish a very tough goal. **Nice job!"**

- "Outstanding news! This will surely build your gross sales volume and contribute to an increase in market share!"

- "Dave has many strengths, including being a motivated self-starter ... He is well organized, trustworthy, conscientious..."

- "...Above is a great job by the **Best in the Business.** You!"

- "Bazooka 10 pack sets a new standard for gum sales in the Columbus market...#1 in unit sales! Great job by Dave Jones and his team at CMI Brokerage!"

- "Dave, pour it on! Great job at Acme. It goes to show, persistence and hard work pays off. Blow your budget away!"

- "...Very well organized, thorough, dedicated..."

- "Dave's maturity, thoughtfulness, and good judgment have created a leadership record for him, engendering the respect of his reportees, as well as other managers..."

- "Dave, great job!! You're making- a large contribution very fast!!! Thanks for a great job!"

- "...Handled his duties with outstanding professionalism."

- "Great job and great follow up. It's really a pleasure to have a pro like you on the team..."

Request For Letter of Recommendation

813 Waynesboro Drive
Tampa, FL 32222

April 7, _____

Jeff Potter, CFO
Southeast Distributors
731 Dillard Square, Building 73
St. Petersburg, FL 32111

Dear Jeff:

Would you be so kind as to write a letter of recommendation to what may well become my future employer? I know you're very familiar with my work, and especially the many professional development activities we've been involved in over the past ten years.

I've been interviewing for CFO positions with several companies in Atlanta—an area where Kathy and I have decided to relocate to in order to be closer to Kathy's mother who lost her husband in January. The company requesting letters of recommendation is Georgia's largest paper products distributor, Tristate Distributors, with revenues in excess of $600 million a year. The letter should be addressed to:

> Sherry Strayer
> Human Resources Department
> Tristate Distributors
> 2871 Highway 24 North
> Atlanta, GA 35555

The responsibilities of this position are very similar to your current responsibilities at Southeast Distributors. Tristate is expecting the new CFO to provide major leadership in developing a new integrated cost accounting system.

Please let me know if you have any questions concerning the position or company. I appreciate your assistance and look forward to perhaps seeing you in Atlanta in the very near future!

Sincerely,

Gary Nelson

Gary Nelson

Requesting Information on a Company

211 Meander Road
Denver, CO 81111

September 3, _____

Stacy Marcella
Account Executive
M. L. Brokers
37 Tower Avenue
Denver, CO 81100

Dear Stacy:

I've been trying to get information on a company in Chicago called Century Finance Corporation. I noticed they are listed on the NASDAQ but I've had difficulty finding much information on them. I've tried several standard sources on the Internet but with little luck.

Would you have access to an annual report or any other type of information that would help me better understand the company and its operation? I'm especially interested in their overall financial health and projected future performance. I'm assuming you have access to information sources that are beyond my reach.

I appreciate your assistance.

Sincerely,

David Mathews

David Mathews

P.S. Thanks for that great tip on Econo Electronics. It just went up five points!

Seeking Additional Information About a Position

95 King George Drive
Chicago, IL 63897

July 23, _____

George Mason, CEO
Stevens and Stevens Co.
36 Raceway Drive
Springfield, IL 61111

Dear George:

A representative of Davis Morgan Company contacted me about their CEO position. The opportunity intrigues me. I'm one of three candidates they will be interviewing during the next three weeks. While I'm familiar with their operations, I'm less informed about the CEO position.

I believe you know the current CEO, Jim Bass, who has been with Davis Morgan for only two years. Is there anything I should know about his work or the position? Do you know why he is leaving?

I'll give you a call the first of next week. I would appreciate any information or insights you might have into this position.

Sincerely,

Bill Ronner

Bill Ronner

Clarifying Questions Raised During an Interview

991 Graystone Avenue
Richmond, VA 26654

October 11, _____

Muriel Sutherland
Vice President of Management
Prudential Industries
246 American Way
Norfolk, VA 23456

Dear Ms. Sutherland:

Thanks again for the opportunity to interview for the Senior Executive Management position. I very much enjoyed meeting with you and your staff and learning more about Prudential Industries, the Norfolk area, and your Latin American market.

I'm still very interested in the possibility of joining Prudential Industries as one of your senior managers. You mentioned my responsibilities would include sales and marketing for your Latin American market. While I'm excited about developing this market, I have a few additional questions that would give me a better idea of how I can best approach this market:

- Which countries do you see as most important to Prudential's growth?
- How many days per year would I expect to travel to the region?
- What kind of local staff assistance would be available?
- To what extent have you achieved your sales goals in this region?
- What are some of the major problems facing Prudential in this market?
- Who is your competition and what do you see as their major strengths?

I'll call you on Tuesday morning to see if you have a few minutes to discuss these questions. I would appreciate your insights into what I consider to be one of the most exciting markets in the coming decade.

Sincerely,

Doug Westerly

Doug Westerly

Withdrawing From Consideration

103 Germantown Road
Tucson, AZ 88888

March 22, ⸺

Thomas Ferris
Port West Enterprises
934 Ocean Drive
San Diego, CA 91111

Dear Mr. Ferris:

After careful consideration, I've decided to accept the position of Director of Operations with Berry Transportation Company in Oklahoma City.

I want to thank you and your staff for considering my candidacy. Post West Enterprises is a very attractive company. However, at this stage in my career, I believe the position I've accepted with Berry Transportation is a better fit.

Best wishes.

Sincerely,

Geraldine Celistine

Geraldine Celistine

Announcing the Acceptance of a Position

883 North Pine
Birmingham, AL 39999

May 3, ———

Doug Carter
4590 Drake Avenue
Charlotte, NC 33333

Dear Doug:

I want to thank you for your support during my recent job search. I'm sure your letter of recommendation was most helpful.

I'm happy to announce that I've accepted a position with Marion Packaging Company in Memphis. Jan and I will be moving to Memphis next month. My first day at Marion begins on May 25th.

This is a very exciting opportunity for me. Working with a 10-person staff, I'll be in charge of sales and marketing in Georgia, Florida, Tennessee, Kentucky, South Carolina, and North Carolina. Perhaps we can get together during my bimonthly trips to North Carolina.

Again, I really appreciate your assistance. I'm sure it made a difference in landing the job!

Sincerely,

Daryl Morgan

Daryl Morgan

4

THE HALDANE WAY:
METHODS, MEDIUMS, AND MESSAGES

What's so different about a Haldane letter? A Haldane letter is based upon a very clear set of career management principles developed by Dr. Bernard Haldane more than 50 years ago. These principles are the foundation of modern career counseling. Successfully incorporated in the job searches of more than 600,000 Bernard Haldane Associates' clients, these principles also have been used by thousands of professional career counselors who have used the Haldane methods in assisting hundreds of thousands of others in developing a successful job search. These are proven methods that are as relevant today as they were more than 50 years ago when Dr. Bernard Haldane revolutionized career counseling theory and practice.

DOING LAST THINGS FIRST

For most people, job finding is no fun. If it were, you would probably be doing it more often and with greater enthusiasm. It's especially no fun if you've just lost your job and are forced to go out and find a new job. Since most peoples' identity is closely aligned with their work and job, being without a job can be very ego-deflating and lonely. Your whole sense of self-worth gets tied up with what you do for a living; all of a sudden you may feel like a nobody since nobody seems to be interested in you. When you go job hunting, you have to explain to strangers that you really are somebody who is worth a lot more than they may think you are worth. More often than not, you must first explain on paper—in the form of a resume and cover letter—why you should be interviewed for a job.

So what do you do? If you are like most people, you've learned how to do a job but never how to find a job. Unfortunately, most people go about the job finding process by doing last things first—they literally start by writing a resume and then send it, along with a cover letter, to job prospects. When asked what they first need to do in order to find a job, the typical answer is to first write their resume. When asked how they plan to write their resume, they usually say they will summarize their work history and education since that's what goes on most resumes. In fact, many job seekers get advice from well-meaning friends and colleagues who loan them a copy of their resume which is organized very similarly—names of employers, inclusive employment dates, a summary of duties and responsibilities, educational background, and personal information. When sending their resume to prospective employers, they then preface their resume with a short cover letter indicating that their resume is enclosed for the employer's consideration. They engage in few job search activities other than send resumes and cover letters in response to classified employment ads.

What's wrong with this picture? It's repeated by thousands of job seekers each day who believe they are doing what's expected in a job search—send resumes and cover letters in response to job ads. However, the quality of their resumes and letters leave a great deal to be desired because they are based upon doing last things first rather than doing first things first. By immediately writing a resume that merely reflects their work history, education, and personal information, they create an obituary—their correspondence is usually dead upon arrival. Such a resume, as well as the accompanying cover letter, tells the employer nothing about the individual's goals and accomplishments. Focusing on the individual's past work history, the writing exercise reveals nothing about what the individual can do for the employer. Indeed, most such resumes and letters paint a picture of an individual who really doesn't know what he or she really wants to do, can do, and will do for the employer. Not surprisingly, few employers are interested in interviewing individuals who communicate their qualifications so poorly.

> **Client Feedback**
>
> *"My enhanced resume and cover letter got me the interview."*
>
> —M.F.

DOING FIRST THINGS FIRST

If you subscribe to the philosophy that you should find a job that fits well with your particular mix of interests, skills, and abilities—one you do well and really enjoy doing—then you must do first things first, which is not writing a resume and cover letter. The Bernard Haldane career management principles are based upon this "fitness" philosophy: you should find a job that is a good "fit" for both you and the employer. And the very first thing you should do is assess your strengths—those things you do well and enjoy doing. With Bernard Haldane Associates, you do this through a self-assessment process called Success Factor Analysis that focuses on analyzing your major accomplishments. As outlined in our companion volume, **Haldane's Best Resumes For Professionals**, this assessment process constitutes the foundation principle of modern career counseling. Once you identify your strengths, you then develop an employer-centered objective that reflects your pattern of accomplishments. All elements in your resume and letters flow directly from this objective. In this sense, writing resumes and letters should be the last things you do—only *after* you have analyzed your accomplishments and formulated an objective.

Individuals who organize their job search by doing first things first tend to present a clear and desirable picture to employers: they have goals; they have a record of accomplishments; their pattern of performance is predictable; they bring value to the position; and they are a perfect "fit" for the position. Individuals who do first things first and present their qualifications accordingly are highly sought after by employers who know exactly what they can and will do for them. Best of all, such individuals find jobs that are extremely rewarding both personally and professionally.

EXPRESSING THE UNIQUE YOU

Whatever you do, make sure your letters reflect the unique you. You do this by focusing on your specific goals and accomplishments. You avoid the canned language of so many typical job search letters that circulate in the job market. You clearly communicate to others that you have a unique mix of interests, skills, and abilities that directly relate to the qualifications desired by the employer. You provide examples of your accomplishments that are unique to your professional experience. In the end, you produce high quality letters that speak the language of employers. Written according to our principles, you write powerful letters that separate you from the crowd of other candidates. Your letters move employers to contact you for a job interview.

PRINCIPLES FOR SUCCESS

Once you know exactly what you do well and enjoy doing, formulate an employer-oriented objective, and write a resume that commands the attention of employers, you are well on your way to producing effective job search communication. Your letters also must incorporate certain principles of success. Above all, they must clearly communicate:

- who you are in terms of skills and accomplishments
- what you want to do

- what patterns of performance you will bring to the job
- what benefits the employer can expect from hiring you

If you are seeking an executive-level position, employers also look for many of these key competencies and qualities:

- leadership
- decision making
- management
- energy
- communication
- problem solving

- teaming
- tenacity
- innovation
- confidence
- meeting deadlines
- developing strategies

In other words, they are looking for high value individuals who can quickly come on board, develop and implement projects, and produce measurable results. They are looking for individuals who have a *demonstrated pattern of success*.

PAPER AND ELECTRONIC MEDIUMS

Should you primarily produce paper or electronic letters and send them by mail, fax, or e-mail? It really depends on the preferences of your letter recipient. Many people prefer receiving resumes and letters by either fax or e-mail because these mediums are easy to access and respond to; they enable recipients to quickly move on to other things. Others prefer receiving letters and resumes through the mail.

Be careful in sending unsolicited faxes and e-mail. Many people still consider these to be private communication channels, similar to private phone lines. Send faxes and e-mail only upon invitation. Otherwise, you may get "shut out" for being presumptuous and wasting the individual's time. The mail remains the acceptable channel for your letters. However, if you are calling your letter recipient before sending them a letter, it's a good idea to ask if they would like you to send your letter by mail, fax, or e-mail. If the individual indicates fax or e-mail, you have an invitation to use what are ostensibly their private channels of communication.

Don't confuse the medium with the message and thus neglect to focus on what's really important—the quality of your message.

Faxes and e-mail are often responded to more quickly than mailed letters. On the other hand, some studies show that letter recipients respond more quickly to mailed letters than to e-mail. Indeed, e-mail has become the bane of many companies where some employees need to spend one to two hours each day just responding to their e-mail. Many of them manage their e-mail by "trashing" unsolicited e-mail.

Please don't confuse the medium with the message and thus neglect to focus on what's really important at this stage in your job search. None of these media is inherently superior to the others. Each has its advantages and disadvantages. Your focus should be on the *quality of your message* vis-a-vis the needs of the employer rather than on the medium through which you convey your message and attempt to "impress" the employer. Keep in mind that you can mix several "dress for success" elements, such as paper color and quality and the delivery method, with your message when you send a letter. These elements disappear when you fax or e-mail a letter. If your letter is electronically scanned for keywords, your choice of language in developing your message becomes just as important as the message itself.

When you write a Haldane letter, your goal is to grab and sustain the reader's attention and move him or her to action. You can best do this by crafting a very persuasive message that focuses on your unique goals and accomplishments which you've identified through Success Factor Analysis. A powerful message, whether it's sent by mail or e-mail, should lead to action on the part of the letter recipient. In the end, a letter is a letter is a letter. You are what you write. Just make sure you are conveying a powerful message that speaks about your goals and accomplishments as well as accurately represents the unique you.

5

STRUCTURE, STYLE, AND CONTENT

The structure, style, and content of your letters should follow several principles of good business communication. If you are to present your best professional self, your letters should adhere to the many rules identified in this chapter. These rules deal with several basic structural elements, such as the use of salutations, enclosures, and postscripts, to more stylistic concerns, such as designing fully-blocked, square-blocked, modified-blocked, or semi-blocked letters. These rules also deal with the choice of language and phrases to best convey your message. Taken together, these rules deal with a variety of questions raised by letter writers concerning how they should best craft and present their message on paper.

LETTER STYLES

Many letter writers neglect the importance of style and thus produce unattractive letters that literally distract from the central message being conveyed in the letter. The message is often crammed in small type at the top of the page with very narrow margins. Such unattractive letters communicate an overall impression of being unprofessional.

You should select a standard letter style that includes proper indenting, spacing, and centering on the page. The four basic styles include:

- semi-blocked
- fully-blocked
- square-blocked
- modified-blocked

Examples of each style appear on pages 71 and 72. The **semi-blocked style** is probably the most widely used letter style. In this case, all paragraphs are indented, usually by five spaces; the date line, salutation, and signature/name appear right of center and near the right margin; and the remaining elements are flush to the left margin.

With the **fully-blocked style**, all letter elements begin on the left side. Since no elements are indented, this letter style also is perfect for e-mail; compose it in your word processing program, paste it in your e-mail program, and transmit it.

The **square-blocked style** follows the same pattern as the fully-blocked style, except in this case the date line is indented near the right margin.

The **modified-blocked style** also follows a similar left flush pattern except for three elements that appear near the right margin: date line, salutation, and signature/name.

LAYOUT AND DESIGN

The layout and design of your letter should be relatively conservative. Avoid fancy fonts and extensive use of italics, bold, and graphic elements. When listing items or emphasizing several points, indent five spaces and start each line with bullets (•) or boxes (■):

■ _____

■ _____

■ _____

■ _____

If your letter accompanies your resume, ideally you should use the same typing font and size so your letter matches your resume. Times Roman, Bookman, Palatino, and Helvetica or similar font styles in 10 to 12 point size work well for letters. Avoid smaller size fonts since they may be hard to read.

Your letter should have an overall balanced look—centered left to right and top to bottom—with margins running from 1" to 1½." Avoid lines that are more than 6" long and run more than 80 characters. Longer lines and more condensed type tend to be more difficult to read. The real test of a letter is how pleasing it is to the human eye. In other words, does it immediately draw the reader to your message and invite him or her to read your letter in depth?

ANATOMY OF A LETTER

The internal structure of your letter will vary depending on your purpose. In general, however, most business letters incorporate these basic elements:

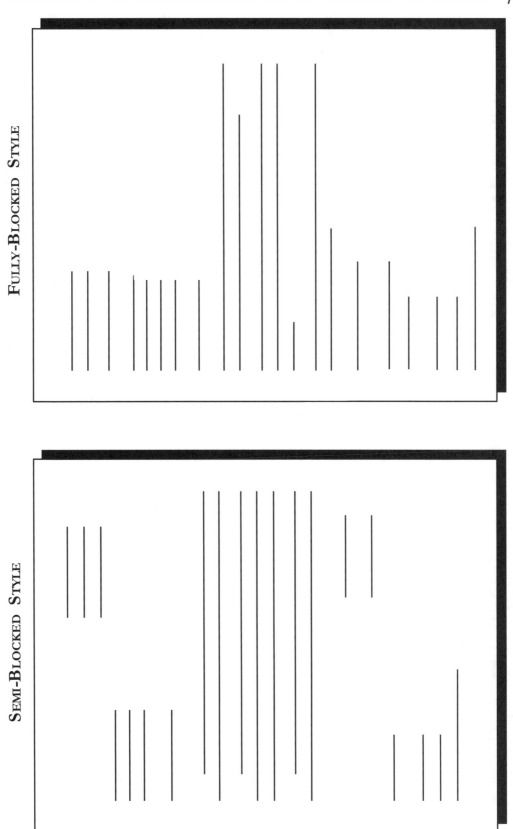

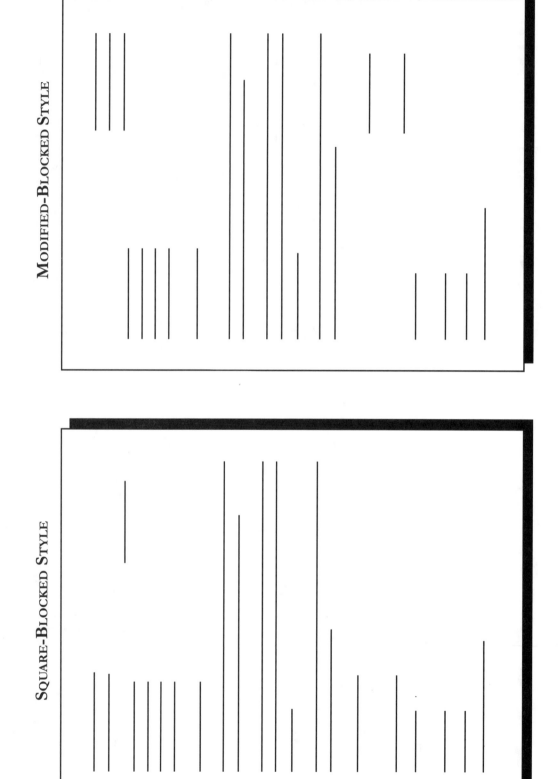

1. Heading
2. Date line
3. Inside address
4. Salutation or greeting
5. Body of letter
6. Closing
7. Signature line
8. Identification initials
9. Enclosures
10. Copy reference
11. Postscript (P.S.)

The first seven elements are mandatory for all business letters; the final four elements are optional, depending on your particular situation. Each of the elements should appear in sequence according to our semi-blocked style example on page 71. Let's examine each of these elements and identify a few rules you should follow when writing your own letters.

1. Heading

The heading usually consists of two to three lines that specifies your mailing address. It informs the reader of your current location as well as provides the necessary information to contact you by mail. You also may want to include your e-mail address immediately following the city, state, and zip code:

> 3781 Tampico Way
> San Francisco, CA 94155
> csmith@aol.com

For mailing addresses, it is preferable to abbreviate the name of your state. In our example, California becomes CA.

If you use preprinted stationery that incorporates a header with your name and address, it's not necessary to repeat this header element. Go directly to the date line instead.

2. Date Line

Skip one line after the header and type the date of your letter. Spell out the month rather than abbreviate it numerically:

> June 21, 1999

3. Inside Address

This section includes the name and address of the letter recipient. Leave at least three lines between the date line and these elements. Include the letter recipient's full contact information:

Janet E. Fuller
Director of Finance
Siliton Management Systems
4734 Greenwood Parkway, Suite 33
Boulder, CO 83421

4. Salutation or Greeting

Leave at least three lines between the last line of the inside address and the salutation. You should always attempt to address your letter to a specific name and use a proper formal salutation that starts with "Dear" and is punctuated with a colon. Address the individual by his or her proper gender, marital status, or professional title. For men, always use Mr. or a professional title, such as Dr.:

Dear Mr. Fuller:
Dear Dr. Fuller:

For women, use the marital neutral Ms. or the marital specific Miss or Mrs. If the individual has a professional title, such as Doctor, the title should supersede these other greetings:

Dear Ms. Fuller:
Dear Miss Fuller:
Dear Mrs. Fuller:
Dear Dr. Fuller:

Unless you are especially close to the individual, avoid using the very familiar first name or variations thereof, such as:

Dear Janet:
Hi Janet:
Janet:

In a job search, you need to maintain a proper professional distance between you and the employer. Consequently, stay with standard business salutations.

There may be an occasion when you need to send a letter to someone but you don't know the name. In writing such "blind letters," the tendency is to create a blind salutation, such as "Dear Sir," "To Whom It May Concern," "Dear Sir/ Madam," or to the position, such as "Dear Director of Marketing." Whatever your choices, do not use "Dear Sir" since the letter recipient may well be of the female gender. "To Whom It May Concern" is overworked. Avoid silly or presumptuous blind salutations, such as "Dear Gentlepeople," "Dear Future Employer," or "Dear Friend." These will not endear you to the reader who does not share your hopes. We prefer using "Dear Sir/Madam," the position ("Dear _____:"), an attention line (ATTN: _____), or a combined position and subject line:

Dear Director:

SUBJECT: Senior Marketing Position

Better still, you may want to omit the salutation altogether. In fact, if you leave out the salutation in a blind letter, it will most likely find its way to the right person without offending someone in the process. The position or department will appear in the inside address. In other words, follow the old adage *"when in doubt, leave it out."*

5. Body of Letter

The body of your letter should contain a polite yet powerful message designed to quickly motivate the reader to take action. Divide the body of your letter into three or four simple, focused, and energetic paragraphs. A single paragraph tends to be too condensed to convey three or four key thoughts that should be included in your letter. Above all, the body of your letter must be a quick read that makes the reader pause to invest more time in you. Keep in mind that, similar to your resume, your letter is likely to be quickly scanned or skimmed rather than slowly read word for word, thought for thought. While you may spend a great deal of time crafting each word, phrase, and paragraph on the assumption that the reader will consume everything you say, in reality, your reader will probably spend no more than 20 to 30 seconds scanning the letter for key thoughts and words. In so doing, he or she may only read 30 percent of what appears in your letter. But if the opening sentence and paragraph are particularly engaging, the reader may decide to invest more time in consuming your letter. Knowing this, your paragraphs should evolve as follows:

- The first paragraph should grab attention by way of connecting you to the reader. The very first sentence should function similarly to a good news headline—it grabs attention and generates enough interest to motivate the reader to invest more time in reading the rest of your letter.

- The second paragraph should emphasize your key accomplishments in relationship to the employer's needs. These need to be specific, reinforced with statistics and examples.

- The third and fourth paragraphs move from accomplishments to actions. Specify what actions you desire and what action you plan to take by requesting an interview as well as specifying that you will soon (state the exact time) follow-up this letter with a phone call.

Each paragraph should encompass a separate but related idea. When writing each paragraph, try to observe the following rules:

- Keep focused on your central purpose and avoid including extraneous information that does not reinforce your central purpose or which raises questions about your professionalism.

- Keep the content interesting, energetic, and active by using lots of action verbs. Speak to your reader as if you were in a face-to-face conversation.

- Keep each paragraph relatively short—a total of five lines with two or three sentences per paragraph. Lengthy paragraphs are uninviting to the reader.

- Keep each sentence relatively short—25 words or fewer per sentence. Long sentences are often difficult to follow, awkward, and irritating, especially if they require re-reading.

While you should keep your letter to a single page, if your letter runs more than one page, be sure to include a page number and your name at the top of the next page.

6. Closing

You can close your letter with several different closings. The first four examples are standard closings used in most job search letters:

Sincerely,
Sincerely yours,
Yours truly,
Very truly yours,
Cordially,
Cordially yours,
Faithfully,
Faithfully yours,
Respectfully,
Respectfully yours,

Depending on the purpose of your letter, you may want to use less conventional closings. If, for example, you are requesting information, you may want to end with one of these closings:

> Gratefully,
> Hopefully,
> Requesting your assistance,
> Waiting anxiously for your reply,
> Thanking you in advance,
> Appreciatively,
> With warmest regards,

If you are turning down a job offer or withdrawing your candidacy, try one of these less conventional closings:

> So happy to have met you,
> Wishing my situation were different,
> So sorry to pass on this,
> Perhaps some other time,
> Apologetically,
> Regretfully,

Such nonconventional closings give letters more personality than the typical letter that closes with a standard closing phrase.

7. Signature Line

Be sure to both type and sign your letter immediately following the closing statement. Your typed name should appear four lines below the closing statement. If you have not included your telephone number elsewhere in your letter, do so immediately following your typed name. For example,

> Sincerely,
>
> *Steve Foster*
>
> Steve Foster
> Tel. 717-823-9112

If you use stationery that preprints your name and address at the top, it's not necessary to type a signature line. Just sign your name after the closing.

Be careful in sending the wrong messages with your signature line and namesake. Try to minimize communicating extreme professional relationships—being too close or too distant. If you only sign your first name, you may be getting too close. In our example, "Steve Foster" should be signed "*Steve Foster*" and not just

"*Steve*." You become known as "Steve" after you have established a relationship—by phone, letter, or in person. If Steve's namesake is "J. Steven Wentworth Foster III," he should consider sharing this unique name at some later date and as part of an interesting employee story—but not at the bottom of his job search letters. For now, this name would appear too formal and distant to most readers who might consider him a strange person with such a name (*"What will we have to call him? How will our clients respond to such a character? Is he weird?"*). By shortening it to "Steve Foster," the writer does not raise unnecessary questions about his personality and professional style.

If you have a professional title, such as Doctor or Ph.D., do not over-formalize your signature line by putting "Dr." before your first name. Instead, insert your abbreviated credentials after your last name:

Steve Foster, M.D.
Steve Foster, Ph.D.

Some people read a lot into the strength and style of a signature. When signing your name, be sure to sign your name as you have spelled it out on the signature line. Ideally, you should have a strong and classy signature that indicates you are a well organized, decisive, and busy person.

Sign your name in blue ink since blue ink contrasts nicely with the black print of your letter.

8. Identification Initials

This first optional letter element should only be used if someone else has transcribed and/or typed your letter. It's usually used when a secretary types a letter for the boss. Since you should be typing your own job search letters, inclusion of identification initials does not particularly enhance your letter. If you include them, the proper form is to identify the writer's initials first followed by the initials of the transcriber/typist. In the case of Steve Foster, whose letter would be typed by his secretary Janet Olson, the identification initials would appear as follows:

SF:JO   or   SF/JO

sf:jo   or   sf/jo
SFoster/jo

Steve Foster
jo

9. Enclosures

If you are enclosing items with your letter, such as a resume or samples of your work, be sure to include an enclosure which immediately follows the identification initials. If you only have one enclosure, simply state "Enclosure." If you have more than one enclosure, indicate the number of enclosures, such as "Enclosures 2." Together with the identification initials, your enclosure lines will look like this:

SF/JO
Enclosure

SF/JO
Enclosures 2

10. Copy Reference

In some cases, you may want to send a copy of your letter to other individuals. If you do so, be sure to include a copy reference (cc:) in which you specify to whom you have sent a copy of your letter. For example, if Steve Foster sends a cover letter to Mary Able, the Director of Marketing—who was referred to him by Kimberly Chambers, one of Mary Able's important mentors—it would be both proper and judicious to send Kimberly Chambers a copy of the letter. In this case, the copy reference, along with the identification initials and enclosure line, would appear as follows:

SF:JO
Enclosures 2
cc: Kimberly Chambers

If there are no identification initials nor enclosure line, the copy reference would simply appear as follows, beginning two lines after the signature line:

Sincerely,

Steve Foster

Steve Foster

cc: Kimberly Chambers

11. Postscripts (P.S.)

Postscripts are usually used to include additional information or add a separate thought that is best placed at the very end of the letter rather than in the body of the letter. Use postscripts sparingly since they can be double-edged swords. On the one hand, a postscript can be very effective in allowing you to emphasize an important point you decided not to include in the body of your letter. Indeed, some information may be best emphasized as a postscript item:

P.S. I'll be in your area Thursday morning. Would that be a good time to meet?

P.S. I just received notification that my RT-3 patent has been approved!

P.S. Mary Jane sends her warm regards. She hopes to see you in Denver next week.

P.S. We should be finished with the WQC evaluation report this Friday. I'll send you a copy next week.

P.S. Will you be attending the PTSR conference on May 13-15? I'm chairing the panel on "New Directions in e-Commerce For Advertising Agencies."

On the other hand, postscripts can be distracting, indicating a lack of organization and professionalism. Many end up being disconnected afterthoughts that actually weaken your main message. In fact, some people use the postscript as a dumping ground for information they forget to include in the body of their letter! If you forget to include something, revise and reprint your letter. A postscript should result in giving added punch to your message. You'll need to judge this one on your own since there are no hard and fast rules for using postscripts. Our recommendation: make sure your postscript adds value to your central message rather than distracts your reader. It should be an integral part of your letter that further motivates the reader to both remember you and invest more time in you.

If you include a postscript, it should start two lines below the previous section on your letter. In fact, the postscript should be the very last item appearing on your letter.

THE SPECIAL CASE OF E-MAIL

If you're sending your letters by e-mail, make sure they conform to the requirements of your e-mail program. The following rules generally apply to e-mail:

1. **Only e-mail a letter and resume if requested to do so by the recipient.** Unwelcomed e-mail may be viewed as an inappropriate intrusion into the recipient's professional and personal life.

2. **Use an attention-grabbing subject line.** Remember, many people receive and discard lots of e-mail each day. Only a few messages—those deemed important—actually get scanned and read. People with high volume e-mail will automatically eliminate messages based on the subject line. Make sure your subject line motivates the reader to open your message. If your e-mail is in response to a request, use this simple line: "Information you requested."

3. **Include complete contact information at the end of your message.** This should consist of your name, mailing address, telephone number, fax number, and e-mail address.

4. **Observe proper letter writing etiquette.** The fact that you are sending a letter by e-mail is no excuse to address the recipient any differently than you would in a regular letter. Unless you know the letter recipient very well, avoid using familiar e-mail salutations such as "Hi John" or a first name. The e-mail culture of short two and three line cryptic messages does not apply to job search letters.

5. **Focus on the content of your message.** Similar to a regular letter, divide your e-mail message into three to four well focused paragraphs. Like regular letters, most readers scan their e-mail rather than read messages word for word.

6. **Separate each paragraph by one line**, similar to a regular letter. Avoid merging your message into a single paragraph. Separate thoughts need to be separated by paragraphs.

7. **Be sure to proofread and spell-check for errors.** It may be more convenient to compose your letter and make all necessary corrections in a word processing program (no margins, indenting, or special effects, such as bold, italics, or bullets) and then paste it into your program. If your e-mail program includes a spell-check function, be sure to use it.

Above all, don't operate on the assumption that e-mail is superior to faxes and regular mail. Recent studies show that e-mail is less likely to get responded to than regular mail. In the end, the only effective letters are the ones that get read and responded to. Most people open envelopes that don't look like junk mail, but these same people don't necessarily open all of their e-mail, especially if they routinely receive 100 to 200 messages a day. The first step to being an effective letter writer is to get your mail opened! Whether it gets scanned or read in depth is another question altogether.

LANGUAGE

Your choice of language should communicate to the reader that you are an interesting, competent, and energetic professional. You can communicate these qualities by doing the following:

1. **Keep your letter reader-centered rather than self-centered.** Avoid repeated reference to yourself as "I" or "my." Instead, focus on the

needs of the reader by referring to "you," "your," and "the company." Remember the "Golden Rule" of writing: *you want to communicate what it is you will do for others rather than what you want them to do for you.*

2. **Use action verbs and the active voice which energizes your writing.** Avoid the passive voice which removes you from action and makes you sound less than enthusiastic. For example, contrast these two statements:

> **Passive:** Production was expanded by 32 percent over a two-year period.
> **Active:** Expanded production by 32 percent within two years.

If you use the passive voice, the reader has difficulty knowing what you did. The language of action verbs and the use of the active voice are ideal for writing about your accomplishments and injecting energy into your writing; you basically sound like you are in charge of getting things done. The active voice follows this very familiar grammatical pattern of subject, transitive verb, and direct object:

Subject	Transitive Verb	Direct Object
I	administered	programs
I	designed	studies
I	directed	teams
I	expanded	markets
I	generated	revenue
I	negotiated	contracts
I	organized	studies
I	recruited	key personnel
I	reduced	costs

However, omit the subject (I) if listing your accomplishments.

3. **Inject energy, enthusiasm, and personality into your writing.** Let the reader know that you are someone he or she will probably like meeting in person, someone who is more than just another job seeker interested in networking for information and job contacts. For example, contrast these two statements in an approach letter which could be written by the same person but from very different perspectives concerning the message being communicated:

Letter #1

John Nelson recommended that I contact you concerning my interest in pursuing new opportunities in research and development. I would like to meet with you to discuss possible job opportunities for someone with my background. I'm enclosing my resume for your reference.

Letter #2

John Nelson was right. Your work at Abbot Labs in re-engineering research and development was brilliant. I know because I closely watched the changes that took place there when I was Director of Research at BioTech Futures. In fact, using your model, we benchmarked our turnaround within eight months. Shortening the new product development cycle by 35 percent, the changes enabled us to remain exceptionally competitive. I'm excited about the possibility of further shortening the cycle by another 25 percent with a company that would be interested in some new and innovative research procedures I've developed over the past six months. Could we meet?

Which of these two letters most appeals to you? While both letter writers establish common ground through their connection with John Nelson, the second letter speaks directly to the interests of the letter recipient and expresses a genuine sense of energy and enthusiasm. This is not a standard formula letter. The writer took the time to customize its contents around the interests of the recipient. Chances are the recipient will perceive a very interesting and talented individual behind the second letter.

6

PRODUCING THE
PERFECT LETTER

O nce you've finished writing the perfect letter, it's time to turn your attention to important production issues. How will you produce your letters? What type of equipment will you use? What type style and type size works best? What about the color, quality, and size of your stationery? And then there's always the question about the envelope. What size, color, and quality envelope should you use?

PRODUCTION EQUIPMENT

The issue of production equipment is easy to deal with—use the best to look your best. You should word process your letters and print them with a letter quality printer. Anything less than letter quality is likely to look unprofessional and amateurish. Typewriter-produced letters make you look like you haven't gotten on the technological curve during the past ten years. A letter printed on a less than letter-quality printer does not communicate class. If you can't type, if you're not computerized, or if you lack a letter quality printer, by all means find someone who can do this work for you. You simply must project your best professional image in your letters because you literally make your first impression through this writing form; therefore, your letters must look first class. There are no excuses for not presenting your best self in all phases of the letter writing, production, and distribution processes.

TYPE STYLE AND SIZE

Choose a standard type style and size that complements your resume and is easy to read. In most word processing programs, Times, Times Roman, Times New Roman, Bookman, New Century, Courier, and Palatino represent standard type styles. Avoid Helvetica, Gothic, Script, and italicized and unconventional styles which are usually difficult to read and often irritating to the reader.

A 10 to 12 point type size works well with most standard type styles. Anything above or below these preferred sizes will tend to be too small or too large. Avoid trying to squeeze a two-page letter on to one-page by dropping the point size below 10 point and/or narrowing your margins. Either edit your letter so it fits on to one page or let it go to two pages. Again, you want to present your best professional image which means selecting a type style and size that is most appealing to the eye.

MARGINS AND CENTERING

Set your margins to 1" to 1½" inches, left to right and top to bottom. A good rule of thumb is that the text of your letter, from left to right on an 8½" x 11" page, should not exceed 6" when the type style is sized at 11 points or less. Long text lines in a 10 to 12 point or smaller type size are difficult to read.

The overall appearance of your letter should be one of balance. You achieve such balance by centering your letter on the page. For example, the distance between the top margin and the first word on the page should be the same as the distance between the bottom margin and the last word on the page.

JUSTIFICATION, HYPHENS, PARAGRAPHS

Set your word processor to left justified. The right-hand margin should be unjustified or ragged edge. Fully justified letters look too formal and mass produced. Avoid breaking words along the right-hand margins with hyphens. Always double-space between paragraphs.

PAPER SIZE AND QUALITY

It's best to use the same size paper as your resume—8½" x 11". Some people recommend using monarch size paper because it stands out from the crowd of other standard sized letters. We can find no evidence that this type of paper makes a positive difference in how employers respond to candidates. In fact, it may communicate the opposite message—you are less than professional in your business communication.

Select a paper color and quality that both looks and feels professional and complements your resume. Similar to paper choices for resumes, our first choice of paper color for letters is white. Since more and more employers electronically scan resumes, white paper works best for scanners. Resumes printed on colored paper may be rejected by some scanners. If your resume is printed on white paper, use white paper for your cover letter as well.

> *Our first choice of paper color is white. Resumes printed on colored paper may be rejected by some scanners.*

If you decide to go with a colored paper, your best choices will be a very light gray, ivory, or off-white paper. Some executive candidates report favorable responses to a white paper with a one-inch gray margin left to right and top to bottom. It definitely stands out from the crowd.

The weight and quality of your paper should be 20 to 60 pound with a 100% cotton fiber or "rag content." A subtle texture looks professional. However, avoid very heavy and textured papers which feel coarse or rough. Most major office supply stores carry good quality paper appropriate for producing professional looking resumes and letters.

ENVELOPES

If you choose to mail your letter in a No. 10 business envelope, your letter should be on the same paper color and quality as the envelope. However, you may want to use a 9" x 12" envelope since it presents your letter and resume flat. Folded resumes and letters are harder to sort and scan than flat ones. If you use a 9" x 12" envelope, it's not necessary that the envelope paper match your letter and resume. In fact, you may want to send your correspondence letter in a cardboard Priority Mail envelope available through the U.S. Postal Service. It only costs $3.20 to send and the red, white, and blue graphics may get the attention of the recipient. However, keep in mind that the only person you may be impressing with such an envelope is a mailroom clerk or secretary who is responsible for opening and sorting the mail, throwing away the envelope, and then passing the contents on to the intended reader who never sees the envelope. In the end, your choice of envelopes may not make such a big impression after all!

7

DISTRIBUTING IT RIGHT

Your letters are only as good as the quality of your distribution activities. If they are to produce desired results, your letters must get into the right hands to get read, remembered, and responded to. Without a good letter distribution plan, your whole job search campaign may go awry.

So what do you plan to do with your letters? Whom will you send them to? How will you send them? Will you be sending them to specific individuals or do you plan to broadcast them to anonymous readers? Let's answer these questions by focusing on what's really important in the whole letter distribution process.

A PURPOSE AND A PLAN

Haldane letters are designed with both a purpose and a plan in mind. Like everything else you do in your job search, letter distribution should be tied to your marketing plan. Similar to a resume, the purpose of your approach, cover, and thank-you letters should be to *get interviews*, whether they be referral interviews or job interviews. The purpose of your interview follow-up letters should be to *get additional interviews and job offers*. Your letters should unlock doors that lead to the right job for you.

A Haldane marketing plan involves two types of letter writing campaigns aimed at two types of interviews—the referral interview and the job interview. **Referral interviews** have five major purposes:

- To establish rapport.
- To get information.

- To get advice and reaction on product, market, and fit.
- To extend your contact network.
- To be remembered favorably and actively.

In other words, referral interviews should result in acquiring information, advice, and referrals that enlarge both your information base and your network of key job contacts. These interviews are critical for conducting a well targeted job search campaign for uncovering jobs that best relate to your interests, skills, and abilities.

Referral interviews also involve a four-step marketing campaign in which both approach and thank-you letters play critical roles:

1. Send an approach letter.
2. Make a follow-up telephone call to schedule a meeting.
3. Conduct the referral interview.
4. Send a thank-you letter.

The referral interview campaign should always begin with an approach letter and end with a thank-you letter. In the case of both letters, your purpose is to open the doors (with an approach letter) of a strategically important person who will meet with you to discuss your career interests and who will remember you (with a thank-you letter) for future reference. Both of your referral interview letters should be carefully crafted with these job search purposes in mind.

From the perspective of the job seeker, **job interviews** primarily have two purposes: acquire information and get a job offer. Not only does the employer need more information about you *before* offering you the job, you also need more information about the position and company *before* making a decision of whether or not to accept an offer. Consequently, in order to satisfy both parties' decision-making requirements, you need to both ask and answer questions.

The process of getting a job interview usually involves writing and sending one type of job search letter—the cover letter. It also involves sending a thank-you letter immediately following the interview. These before and after job interview letters can make the critical difference between being offered a job interview and a job or being passed over for further consideration.

NAMES AND ADDRESSES

Your letters should always be addressed to a specific individual and to a verified address. If you don't know the person's name, are unclear about the person's gender, have questions about spelling, or are uncertain about an address, by all means make a telephone call to get accurate information. Your marketing plan and letters are too important to be left to chance and errors. If you send your letter to the wrong person, misspell the person's name, or use the wrong address, you immediately make a negative first impression which is difficult, if not impossible, to overcome. You'll probably be seen as someone who lacks attention to detail and makes mistakes.

Once you have a correct name and address, you also will be prepared to conduct a follow-up. Your follow-up is critically important to getting interviews and job offers. By all means do not assume it's the responsibility of the letter recipient to contact you. It is *your* responsibility to make contact with the letter recipient by making follow-up calls. If you fail to do this, you will most likely get no response to your

> *It's your responsibility to make contact with the letter recipient by making follow-up calls.*

letter. If you initially get the correct name, address, and phone number of the letter recipient, you will be prepared to make the critical follow-up call.

TO BROADCAST OR NOT

Consider the mountains of paper and electronic communications thrown at employers each day by individuals who believe in the efficacy of broadcasting their employment interests and qualifications. Take, for example, Microsoft Corporation which attracts hundreds of thousands of broadcasters each year. How do they manage such waves of unsolicited communications? CEO Bill Gates in his book, ***Business @ the Speed of Thought***, reveals how Microsoft copes with this situation:

> We receive 600 to 900 resumes from job applicants every day by postal mail, by e-mail, or via our Resume Builder on the Microsoft Web site. Seventy percent of the resumes arrive electronically via e-mail or the Web, up from 6 percent two years ago and rising. Our software automatically acknowledges every electronic submission. Our recruiting database, from Restrac of Lexington, Massachusetts, directly accepts information from resumes created at our Resume Builder Web site; e-mail submissions are parsed to deliver candidate information to Restrac. A paper resume is scanned and converted into text that can go into the database. All resumes are electronically matched with open job positions within twenty-four to forty-eight hours of receipt.

Other large and technically savvy companies have also gone to automated systems that allow them to scan, store, and retrieve such communication as well as respond to each inquiry with a nice *"thank-you but not right now"* letter. However, many companies still have their employees, which are usually overworked human resources personnel, handle each letter and resume. This often means they lack the capacity to respond to every broadcasted letter and resume as well as store and retrieve them for future reference. More often than not, broadcasted resumes and letters are thrown away because they are a nuisance to these non-automated organizations.

It's always best to target your letter and resume to specific people who have the power to hire. If you decide to broadcast or "shotgun" your letter and resume, don't expect to get positive results other than an occasional *"thank-you but not right now"* letter which should not be interpreted as an encouraging sign of interest. The broadcast activity itself may make you feel good—you're doing something rather than nothing to progress your job search. But the statistical probability of getting an interview from a broadcast letter and resume is less than one percent. You literally need to send hundreds, if not thousands, of such broadcast pieces in order to get a single positive response. This means spending over $1,000 on a modest mailing to land perhaps one interview. If you don't mind such high costs and low returns—and you want to feel good about doing something—then by all means broadcast your letter and resume. You'll probably initially feel good taking all of your mail to the post office—expecting to get lots of responses—and then you'll probably feel depressed three weeks later when no one has invited you to an interview. Since you will be unable to follow-up such a mailing with telephone calls, this broadcast activity lacks follow-up closure that normally increases response rates.

If you decide to broadcast your letter and resume, and you are seeking a job that pays in excess of $50,000 a year, you may want to concentrate on broadcasting your qualifications to headhunters rather than employers. Most headhunters are in the business of collecting resumes so they can market qualified candidates to their clients—employers who use such services. At present the Internet performs this function for headhunters. Indeed, in the past few years, the Internet has become the headhunter's best friend with its more than 3,000 employment sites that are rich with hundreds of thousands of resumes. By posting your resume on several of these Internet sites, you participate in a form of resume broadcasting. However, these sites do not allow you to include a cover letter which may be more powerful than your resume. If you develop a strong broadcast letter and send it directly to thousands of headhunters, you may have a better chance of getting marketed by a headhunter who may not have found you on the Internet. But, again, this is a high cost and low return strategy for getting job interviews.

At Haldane Associates we use a more targeted broadcast method that involves broadcasting mini-profiles rather than resumes or letters of clients' qualifications. We send these mini-profiles to employers who indicate they are in a hiring mode as well as headhunters who request receiving our profiles. We find this broadcast method to be more effective than sending a typical broadcast letter and resume because of the quality of our mailing list—employers currently hiring and headhunters who request our profiles. In contrast to most broadcasted letters and resumes, our profile mailings are not considered junk mail by employers and head-hunters. Nonetheless, we are aware of the limitations of even this type of broad-cast approach. Such an approach can *supplement* a job search but it should never be viewed as a substitute for targeted job search activities like the highly effective referral interview and the "T" letter. Indeed, when you broadcast, you cannot use a powerful "T" letter, because you are not respond-ing to a specific position which outlines required skills and qualifications. At best, you may encoun-ter "dumb luck" with your timing—you stumbled onto a position that just happened to be open when your letter and resume arrived! Some people do experience such dumb luck in their job search. It's part of the serendipity that characterizes many job searches.

In contrast to most broadcasted letters and resumes, our profile mailings are not considered junk mail by em-ployers and head-hunters.

If you decide to broadcast a letter, you may want to do so with another purpose in mind—to get the name of a specific individual whom you can contact with a more targeted ap-proach. Take, for example, a broadcast letter sent to all CEOs or Vice-Presidents of Human Resources of 1000 manufacturing firms. This broadcast letter might result in 150 responses from a variety of individuals who would be responsible for making hiring decisions in your area of expertise. Most of the letters might consist of some version of this polite rejection:

> Thank you for your interest in our company. While we do not have a posi-tion open at present for someone with your qualifications, we will keep your resume on file for future reference.

The most important thing to look for in this response letter is the name and position of the writer. Hopefully, your broadcast letter has resulted in giving you a key contact within the organization. Your next step should be to call or write to this person to set up an informational or referral interview. Accepting that no position is available at present with this company, you're seeking information, ad-vice, and referrals. In so doing, your broadcast letter becomes a "cold call" for expanding your network of contacts.

MAIL, FAX, AND E-MAIL

Unless requested to fax or e-mail your letters, plan to send your letters by mail. More and more employers now request that letters and resumes be sent by fax or e-mail. If faxing a letter, it's not necessary to include a cover fax sheet. Just fax the same letter you would ordinarily send through the mail. If you e-mail a letter, be sure to include an attention-grabbing subject line; assume your recipient receives lots of e-mail, some of which is quickly discarded based on the attention line. If, for example, you are sending a referral approach e-mail, personalize the subject line like this:

Referred to you by Shanna Taylor

If you're sending a letter of application, personalize the subject line like this:

Qualifications requested for marketing position

If you are conducting an international job search and much of your communication is directed to employers abroad, you will probably send most of your letters by fax or e-mail. If you have both the fax number and e-mail address of your letter recipient, you may want to correspond through both channels simultaneously. Since faxes and e-mail sometimes get lost or misplaced and many people access their e-mail while traveling, transmitting simultaneously by both fax and e-mail will ensure that your recipient receives your correspondence. Your e-mail makes it convenient for them to quickly respond to you. Try this combined fax and e-mail follow-up approach. Fax your letter and immediately follow it up with a short e-mail message, which includes a copy of your faxed letter, mentioning that you just faxed a letter. Include the copy in the body of your e-mail rather than as an attachment:

> *Make the 3-Rs of writing—reading, remembering, and responding to you—quick and easy for the letter recipient.*

Dear Mr. Wilson:

Earlier today I faxed you a letter concerning my interest in joining TRI International in Brussels (copy follows). Please let me know if you have any questions. I can be contacted by phone, fax, or e-mail.

Jeffrey Stone
3871 W. Arlington Avenue
Chicago, IL 60333 USA
Tel. 333-333-3333
Fax 333-333-3334
E-mail: StoneJ@aol.com

This approach makes it easy for the recipient to both quickly read and respond to your messages. The point here is to make the 3-Rs of writing—reading, remembering, and responding to you—quick and easy for the letter recipient. The fax and e-mail combination has a much higher probability of getting read, remembered, and responded to than just sending a letter or fax.

If you are requested to fax or e-mail your letter, it's not necessary to send an original copy in the mail. However, it doesn't hurt to do so, since an original mailed copy will function as a subtle follow-up reminder that you recently communicated with the individual by fax or e-mail. If you haven't received a response to your fax or e-mail, the mailed copy may result in a response. Even though you may think your e-mail and fax were received by the recipient, many times such communication gets lost or overlooked. Be sure to indicate at the top of your original letter that you previously faxed or e-mailed the letter:

FAXED 6/9/99

or

E-MAILED 6/9/99

SPECIAL DELIVERY METHODS

If you are mailing a letter and time is of the essence, by all means use a special next-day or second-day delivery method that stands out from the regular mail, such as Federal Express, UPS, or Express Mail, which costs anywhere from $10.00 to $20.00. However, sending your letter in the U.S. Postal Service's two-day red, white, and blue Priority Mail envelope, which only costs $3.20, is just as attention-grabbing as the more expensive next-day and second-day services. The only downside is that two-day Priority Mail is not reliable; it often takes three to four days to get this two-day delivery!

While special mailing services and colorful special mailers do get the attention of letter recipients, we know of no employers who have interviewed and hired someone based on the speed of their letter or the color and design of their envelope. In fact, such mailing methods may send an unintended message if time is not of the essence: you look too eager; you're probably extravagant; or you may become a pest. In most cases, a letter sent by first-class mail in a matching #10 business envelope will be just as effective as letters sent by special delivery services and in large and colorful envelopes. While the medium is important, it is the message you want to communicate. You should focus on the message conveyed in your letter—your qualifications and accomplishments—rather than all the bells and whistles, which may become unnecessary distractions, involved in delivering your message. Remember, employers are looking for employees who can add value to their operations rather than acquire show horses who require expensive upkeep.

8

FOLLOW-UP AND EVALUATION

Writing, producing, and distributing a letter gets your message in front of a potential reader. But these activities in no way guarantee that the reader will take desired actions, such as meet with you for information and advice, invite you to a job interview, or offer you a job. You want your letter recipient to *take action*, whether it's positive or negative. If it's positive, you go on to the next stage of your job search, which hopefully is a job interview or offer. If it's negative, you no longer need to spend time with this prospect; go on to other more promising opportunities. What you want is a *response* so you can move on to more fruitful activities. What you don't want is no response whatsoever. No response means you have been ineffective.

WAITING USUALLY MEANS NOTHING HAPPENS

It's really surprising how many job seekers write outstanding letters, produce and distribute them well, and then *wait* to be contacted by the letter recipient. They make a fatal assumption about letter recipients: it's the recipient's responsibility to contact the writer. So they wait, wait, wait, and wait. After waiting a few weeks, they give up, interpret no response as a "no", and then move on to other individuals with whom they repeat the same pattern: wait, wait, wait, and wait. After waiting for so long and with no response, some job seekers conclude that many employers are simply inconsiderate. They at least owe the writer a response!

If you are one of these wait, wait, wait, and wait job seekers, you've yet to bring complete closure to your job search. You also have a very distorted view of reality and of those who are responsible for responding to your letters. You should begin with these two assumptions:

- In the job search, he who waits is lost; proactive people are more likely to get desired responses than reactive or sedentary people.

- It's the letter writer's responsibility to generate a response to the letter.

Waiting simply is not a good job search strategy. Remember, two facts of life about letters and letter recipients:

1. Letter recipients are very busy people who neither have the time nor motivation to respond to all their correspondence, and especially if it is low priority correspondence.

2. Most letter recipients feel no obligation to respond to unsolicited correspondence.

"Getting to one's mail" is a constant problem in today's business world. Indeed, busy people tend to be overextended to the point where they have little time to sit down and compose thoughtful responses to all the correspondence they receive. After handling telephone calls and meeting people all day, the last things that get done tend to be reading and writing letters.

The lack of response from your letter recipient can mean several things:

- Didn't receive your correspondence or can't remember receiving it.

- Received your letter but has been ill, out of town, or on vacation for the past two weeks.

- Received your correspondence but hasn't had time to read *and* respond.

- Received and read your correspondence but hasn't had time to respond.

- Received, read, and decided not to respond because of uncertainty about being positive or negative at this time.

- Not interested in speaking or meeting with you right now.

- Not interested in speaking or meeting with you now or in the future.

If you get no response, it means you have yet to motivate the letter recipient to take action—you need to make a phone call!

If you wait and get no response, it's safe to assume nothing is likely to happen. This does not mean the letter recipient is not interested in you. It just means you have yet to move this individual to take action. A letter does not move people to action; at best, it's an invitation to take action. A phone call or a personal visit may result in action, but a letter by itself is not likely to move someone to take action.

TAKING TIMELY ACTION

If you sit back and wait, chances are you will get no response even though the individual may be interested in you. Therefore, it is incumbent upon you to be very proactive at this stage of your job search. You simply must follow-up if you want your letter recipient to take action. It's *your* responsibility—not the letter recipient's—to take action.

Always write your letter with a specific follow-up action in mind. Take, for example, these two standard closings for a letter:

Thank you for your consideration.

I look forward to hearing from you.

These closings, in effect, inform the letter recipient that you will not be calling them; they have a choice of either contacting you or not contacting you. And what do you think they will do? Not surprisingly, most will not contact you.

On the other hand, if you end your letter by stating what you will do next, chances are you will get action because you took action. Contrast these closing statements with the previous closings:

I'll call your office on Tuesday morning to see if your schedule would permit us to meet briefly within the next week. I look forward to speaking with you on Tuesday.

I know you're very busy. But I would appreciate the opportunity to meet with you for a few minutes to discuss my interests. Would next week be a good time to meet? I'll call you on Tuesday to check your schedule. I appreciate your time.

What do you think happens next? The letter recipient is put on alert that you will be calling on Tuesday morning. He basically has choices in this situation. First, he can prepare to take your call on Tuesday by making certain decisions about what he wants to happen next. Second, he may alert his gatekeepers to stop you at the gate with a message that either encourages or discourages you. Third, he may call you immediately to discuss your letter and perhaps conduct an interview over the phone. Whatever the case, this follow-up statement sets the stage for decisions and actions that can add momentum to your job search.

> *By stating in the letter that you will call at a particular time, you set the stage for speaking directly with the letter recipient.*

You'll soon know what is happening because you will have taken specific follow-up actions.

The most effective follow-up consists of a telephone call to the letter recipient. You should make this call within seven days of sending the letter by mail or within four days of faxing or e-mailing a letter. As noted earlier, make sure you include a follow-up statement near the end of your letter. This statement, in effect, opens the door for making the follow-up call. By stating in the letter that you will call at a particular time, you set the stage for speaking directly with the letter recipient. At the same time, you have taken the initiative to schedule a telephone interview. If you are following-up on an approach letter, this may be an opportunity to conduct an informational/referral interview over the phone or to schedule a face-to-face meeting. If you are following-up on a cover letter in response to a specific position, both you and the letter recipient will be engaged in a screening interview—you screening the employer and the employer screening you.

Making a follow-up call is sometimes easier said than done given the role of gatekeepers and voice mail in today's telephone communication. The key to conducting an effective follow-up is observing the 5-Ps of effective follow-ups. Always be:

- Polite
- Pleasant
- Professional
- Positive
- Persistent

Also, try to be enthusiastic and articulate on the phone. You may, for example, need to make eight phone calls before getting through to the person. This may mean leaving eight messages with a gatekeeper or on voice mail. A typical initial voice mail message might start like this:

> Hi, this is Janet Berry calling in reference to my letter of May 7th. I said I would call you today concerning my interest in learning more about your work in public relations. My number is 765-4321. I look forward to speaking with you soon.

Whatever you do, make sure you remain polite, positive, and enthusiastic with each call. Do not indicate your irritation in not having your phone calls returned. Like responding to the mail, at the end of the day many busy people have lots of messages to return. They must prioritize which ones get called first. If you have 30 messages waiting for you, chances are you may only call the top ten. You know which ones should receive your immediate attention by their name, organization, and/or the nature of their message. Someone who is following up on an approach or cover letter may receive very low priority. You increase your probability of getting a return call if you continue to call back and leave messages every day or two:

> Hi, this is Janet Berry calling again in reference to my letter of May 7th. Sorry I missed you again. My number is 765-4321. I'll be here until 4:00 today and then all day tomorrow from 9 to 5. I look forward to speaking with you soon.

After awhile, the individual recognizes your name. He or she may even feel guilty having not responded to your sixth message! Better still, if you've not received a return call after the fourth message, change your message to include a follow-up statement, such as this one:

> Hi, this is Janet Berry calling in reference to my letter of May 7th. Sorry I missed you again. If you would like to call me, my number is 765-4321. If you don't have an opportunity to call me today, I'll call you tomorrow morning. I look forward to speaking with you.

This statement alerts the individual that you are not going away—you'll be calling again and again and again. The best way to put an end to these persistent messages is to call you back! By stating you will call again at a specific time, you increase your chances of having your phone call returned immediately.

If your message still goes unanswered, at this point you might want to inject some humor in your next message or escalate the urgency of speaking with the individual. For humor, try this type of message:

> Hi, this is Janet Berry calling in reference to my letter of May 7th. Sorry I missed you again. I must be doing something wrong since I haven't been able to get through to you after four phone calls. John Shaw warned me that you were very busy but he said I really should talk with you about my career interests. I'm not trying to sell you anything, I'm not looking for a job, and I'm not really a pest. I'll only take a few minutes of your time. If you would like to call me, my number is 765-4321. If you don't have an opportunity to call me today, I'll call you again tomorrow morning. I look forward to speaking with you.

For urgency, mail a copy of your letter after your fifth unanswered call and then make a final follow-up call and leave this message:

> Hi, this is Janet Berry again. I haven't heard from you yet and I am eager to talk with you. I mailed a copy of my original letter in case my first one missed you somehow. I realize you must be very busy but I am interested in meeting with you. My schedule allows me to meet anytime on May 16th or 19th. If either of these dates work, please confirm a time by calling me at 765-4321. I look forward to meeting you.

Live gatekeepers require a different telephone approach. If you encounter a gatekeeper, such as a receptionist or secretary, your conversation might go like this:

Gatekeeper:	Mr. Germain's office. Marlene speaking. How can I help you?
You:	Hi, this is Janet Berry calling for Mr. Germain.
Gatekeeper:	Mr. Germain is in a meeting. Could I take a message?
You:	Yes. I'm calling in reference to my letter of May 8th in which I mentioned I would be calling today to schedule an appointment. When would be a good time to reach him?
Gatekeeper:	His meeting lasts until 4:00. I'll let him know you called.
You:	It may be more convenient if I called him after 4:00. I'll plan to do that!

Since you may or may not get a return phone call, you lose control by leaving a message. By calling back, you remain in control of this situation. If you call back and the person is not available, repeat the same message:

Gatekeeper:	Mr. Germain's office. Marlene speaking. How can I help you?
You:	Hi, this is Janet Berry calling for Mr. Germain.
Gatekeeper:	Yes, I remember you called earlier. I'm sorry but Mr. Germain's in another meeting. Can I take a message?
You:	When would you expect him to be free?
Gatekeeper:	I think he'll be in the meeting the rest of the day. I know he's free tomorrow afternoon. Can I take a message?
You:	Yes, could you tell him I'll give him a call tomorrow afternoon? Would 3:00 be okay?
Gatekeeper:	I'm not sure, but I'll let him know you'll be calling at that time.
You:	Thanks again. I appreciate your assistance.

If you still have difficulty making contact with this person, make another phone call and be pleasantly persistent. Try to develop a relationship with the gatekeeper who may, in the end, become a good friend and a personal advocate. At this point, the gatekeeper knows you and also knows she has been ineffective in getting her boss to return your call. You may now have a sympathetic ally on your side who will try to help you. Your next conversation might go like this:

| Gatekeeper: | Mr. Germain's office. Marlene speaking. How can I help you? |
| You: | Hi, Marlene. Janet Berry calling again for Mr. Germain. |

Gatekeeper: Hi, Janet. Mr. Germain is in another meeting. I gave him your message and mentioned that you had called before. I know he's extremely busy because of an important project deadline which is tomorrow.

You: Could you please let him know that I called? I'll give him a call again on Thursday afternoon. Do you think that might be a good time to catch him since his project will be over by then?

Gatekeeper: I'll give him the message but I'm not sure about Thursday since I know he's trying to catch up on several other projects he's involved with. I'll mention to him that you will be calling again on Thursday afternoon. It may be best to try around 3:00 since he has no meetings scheduled for that time.

You: Thanks again. I really appreciate your assistance. Hopefully we can connect this time. I'm really looking forward to talking with him since I've heard so much about his fine work in product development at RCR Corporation.

Gatekeeper: Yes, he's one of our real stars here at RCR. I'm sure you'll enjoy speaking with him.

You: I'll give you a call again at 3:00 on Thursday to check on his schedule.

There's a good chance you will connect with this person on Thursday at 3:00 because the gatekeeper is sympathetic to your situation. She probably likes you because you're pleasantly persistent. Indeed, she may put in a good "word" for you with her boss. Her next conversation with her boss might go something like this:

Janet Berry called again for you today concerning her letter of May 8th. I told her you were very busy. She's really looking forward to speaking with you and asked if she could call again on Thursday afternoon. I told her to try around 3:00. Is that okay? Or do you want me to give her a message when she calls? She's a real nice person who is one of your fans. She knows you're very busy and only wants to talk with you briefly.

If you're Janet, chances are you will soon get through to Mr. Germain because of your persistent approach. Had you waited for him to respond to your letter or your first phone call, chances are you would still be waiting. Whether you are communicating with voice mail or a gatekeeper, pleasant persistence usually will eventually pay off.

KEEPING TRACK

Make sure you put together a good record keeping system to both track and retrieve your correspondence. You need a system that helps you conduct regular follow-ups and refer to correspondence when someone contacts you. For follow-up purposes, you may want to organize a 30-day file system in which you move copies of your correspondence to a file date that requires a follow-up call—usually 5-7 days after mailing your letter. Other alternatives include using a day-planner, large calendar, or a software program, such as Sidekick, ACT, or Access to track your activities and remind you of upcoming follow-up activities.

You also should keep a list of your current contacts (name, organization, telephone number, and summary of previous actions) near your telephone. Should you receive a phone call in response to a letter, you can quickly refer to this list to refresh your memory. If an employer calls you and you can't remember what you should be talking about, this could become a very embarrassing conversation. Worst of all, this call will probably be a screening interview. Not knowing with whom you're talking or having to ask questions, such as *"Who are you with? What position is it? What did I send you?"* will leave a very bad impression. You'll sound both disorganized and uninterested in this particular person. If the call comes at a bad time or if you are clueless about this person, ask if you could call them back in a few minutes:

> Thanks for calling. Could I call you back in a few minutes? I'm in the middle of something that I'll be finished with in five minutes. What is your name and phone number?

This statement will buy you some time to get your act together. Immediately check your records for copies of correspondence and other information on the person you will be speaking with shortly. When you call back, you should be well prepared to talk with this person.

EVALUATING YOUR EFFECTIVENESS

As we noted from the very beginning of this book, the only good letters are the ones that get read and responded to in positive ways. Effective letters result in job interviews and offers. While most job search letters get read by someone, few ever get responded to with an invitation to interview. If you want to be most effective in your job search, you must write well focused letters that move individuals to take action. But don't expect the content of your letter alone to result in action. If you wait for a response, chances are you will get no response. Therefore, it is incumbent upon you to follow-up every letter you write. You should never assume the letter recipient will pick up the phone and call you because of your letter. That's simply wishful thinking.

The most effective job seekers are those who are proactive at every stage of their job search. This does not mean they are excessive, pushy, aggressive, or obnoxious. Rather, they are pleasantly persistent, tenacious, and professional in their follow-up approach. And being proactive in writing job search letters means picking up the telephone to speak with the letter recipient concerning the contents of your letter. If you are to be both proactive and effective, evaluate your correspondence according to these criteria:

Follow-Up Actions	**Yes**	**No**
1. Included a follow-up statement at the end of my letter indicating when I would call within the next seven days.	1	0
2. Filed my letter and information on the letter recipient in an action-oriented follow-up file.	1	0
3. Prepared an initial positive and professional voice-mail message as well as a similar message to leave with a gatekeeper.	1	0
4. Observed the 5-Ps of making follow-up calls.	1	0
5. Prepared several questions to ask over the phone which indicate my interest, enthusiasm, and professionalism.	1	0
6. Made the first follow-up call at the time and date I stated in my letter.	1	0
7. Left positive and professional messages each time I made a follow-up call; never indicated any irritation or disappointment in not having my calls returned.	1	0
8. Called at least eight times over a two-week period (no more than once a day) before writing a follow-up letter and moving on to other prospects.	1	0
9. When speaking with the letter recipient, I asked for an interview and scheduled one accordingly.	1	0
10. Followed-up the follow-up call with a nice thank-you letter indicating my sincere appreciation for the person's time and information.	1	0

TOTAL ☐

Add the numbers to the right of each statement. If your total is "10," you're doing a great job in following up your letters; your letters are most likely achieving desired results. If your score is below "10," you need to work on those activities that will improve your job search effectiveness.

9

HALDANE COVER LETTERS

Most Haldane clients come to us with a prepared resume, which a Career Advisor subsequently helps the client restructure so it conforms to the principles of Haldane resumes. But few clients also come prepared with letters they need to write at various stages of their job search campaign. Indeed, many of them have never considered how important a cover letter could be to their job search effectiveness. Preoccupied with crafting a resume, they tend to treat letter writing as a pro forma activity.

What letters clients do bring to us are often inappropriate for the type of targeted job search we envision for our clients. In most cases, a Career Advisor works with the client in carefully crafting cover letters along with other types of job search letters. Not surprisingly, two of the most powerful letters our clients write are the "T" letter and Focus Piece. Developed by Bernard Haldane Associates, these unique letters are responsible for generating numerous interviews for our clients. Time and again, our former clients stress how important these letters were in getting interviews and landing a job. Such letters command the attention of potential employers who invite them to interviews.

In this chapter we include numerous examples of job search letters used by our clients, from cover letters to approach and thank-you letters. All are drawn from the files of Haldane clients. These examples should give you a clear picture of what goes into creating a first-class Haldane cover letter. Based on the principles outlined in previous chapters, these letters focus on the candidate's strengths and accomplishments in reference to the employer's hiring needs. Coupled with a powerful Haldane resume, these letters helped shorten our clients' job search time. The clients went on to get interviews and job offers that led to continuing career success.

All names, addresses, and employers have been changed to protect the confidentiality of our clients. Any resemblance to real persons or organizations is purely coincidental.

Direct Approach Letter
To A Friend For A Referral Interview

564 West Street, Apt. 543
Colorado Springs, CO 45621

April 25, _____

Mr. Joe Klein
3345 Rodale Blvd.
Denver, CO 45623

Dear Joe:

As friend to friend, I wanted to let you know that I'm making some plans for the future and thought about you and some of the good times that we have shared in the past. It seemed like a good time to catch up with current events.

All things considered, I've decided to leave Corporate Holdings to pursue a career path more in keeping with my long-range objectives.

In my next job assignment, I want to work for a progressive company with a team approach to problem solving. My specific interests lie in the area of program or plan management…I really like starting something and seeing it through to completion and then starting another project.

Please understand, Joe, that *I'm not expecting you to have a job, nor even know of one.* Instead, I am seeking your advice and insight with regard to my career marketing campaign.

I have always trusted your judgment, Joe, and would very much appreciate any advice and suggestions that you may have. I've enclosed a copy of my resume for your review.

I am really excited about prospects for the future and look forward to discussing them with you. I'll call you on Monday afternoon, February 19, in order to set up a time for getting together for a chat. In the meanwhile, please give my best to Jane.

Warm regards,

Randall Jackson

Randall Jackson

Enclosure

Direct Approach Letter For A Referral Interview

1050 Maryland Ave.
Baltimore, MD 20741

January 31, _____

Dr. Tracy Stanton
Director of Research
Woodland and Spensor Visions Inc.
5823 Westend Road
Baltimore, MD 20748

Dear Dr. Stanton:

Recently I began conducting research into the environmental industry. During this research, it became clear to me that the Woodland and Spensor Visions Inc. company is recognized as a leader in this area. I am writing to you, Dr. Stanton, because of your experience and expertise in the lymnological applications industry and hope you will be willing to share some of that insight with me.

At the present time I am actively seeking a position in applied research. The enclosed resume outlines my objective and supports it with some of my qualifications and achievements.

Please understand, *I do not expect you to have or know of any current openings.* However, I would appreciate a discussion to seek your ideas, suggestions, comments, and reactions on how I might achieve my objective.

Appreciating your time is valuable, I assure you I will keep our meeting brief. I will call you on Thursday, February 16, to arrange an appointment.

Sincerely,

Tricia Moheman

Tricia Moheman

Enclosure

Direct Approach Letter For A Referral Interview

3624 Cypress Avenue
Novak, CA 54628

April 16, _____

Dr. Maximillian Randall
Director of Operations
Data Exchange, Inc.
2156 Advanced Drive
San Jose, CA 54621

Dear Dr. Randall:

I am writing to you because of your well-known expertise in the area of project management and software implementation.

Currently, I am looking for a new career opportunity that will allow me to use proven skills in management, supervision, and system applications. It is my intention to leave the life and health insurance industry and apply my skills in a different private sector business.

Please understand, Dr. Randall, *I am not applying for a position with your company, nor do I expect you to know of any current job openings.* What I seek is information to enable me to decide if my skills and expertise could fit into an organization similar to Data Exchange, Inc.

Enclosed is a copy of my professional profile. When we meet, you may have suggestions about which businesses can offer interesting, challenging, and rewarding career opportunities while using my skills and talents. Also enclosed is a tentative list of questions I would like to discuss with you.

Again, Dr. Randall, I am not asking you for a job, but merely seeking *advice* and information that will help me decide where I should direct my efforts. I will call your office on April 21, to schedule a brief meeting at a time that is convenient for you.

Sincerely,

Dorothy Lyndall

Dorothy Lyndall

Enclosure

Direct Approach Letter For A Position

5430 Stimson Street
Springfield, MA 01106

February 13, _____

Mr. David Hansen
Vice President
Purify Services Inc.
206 Oak Street
Springfield, MA 01104

Dear Mr. Hansen:

In pursuit of a career in the specialty automotive market place, I am searching for a progressive organization to which I can effectively contribute my 10 years experience in automotive marketing, sales management, creative planning, and implementation.

Enclosed is a resume that supports my objective with some of my qualifications and achievements. You will note that I have been especially effective in the areas of market research and strategic planning, most notably in new product roll outs where I implemented marketing plans that helped increase company revenues 57%.

I would like to discuss with you how I am prepared to contribute to Purify Services Inc., and I will call you on Thursday, August 22, to arrange a brief meeting.

Sincerely,

Morgan K. Ashley

Morgan K. Ashley

Enclosure

Direct Approach Letter For A Referral Interview

111 First Street
Boston, MA 02222
July 8, _____

Ms. Joanne Hazlett
VP Sales and Marketing
Ultra Faucet Corp.
78 W. 56th Street
Orono, ME 55231

Dear Ms. Hazlett:

I am writing to you because of your position as Vice
President of Sales and Marketing for Ultra Faucet Corp.

Please understand Ms. Hazlett, I *am not applying for a
position with your company, nor do I expect you to know of
any current job openings.* What I seek is information to
enable me to decide if my skills and expertise could fit
into an organization similar to Ultra Faucet Co.

Currently, I am looking for a new career opportunity that
will allow me to use proven skills in developing territo-
ries, coaching individuals and motivating sales. It is my
intention to leave my current position and apply my skills
in a different private sector business. When we meet, you
may have suggestions about which businesses can offer interesting, challenging, and rewarding career opportunities
while using my skills and talents.

Again Ms. Hazlett I am not asking you for a job, but
merely seeking *advice* and information that will help me
decide where I should direct my efforts. I will call your
office the week of September 28, to schedule a brief meeting at a time that is convenient for you.

Sincerely,

Darlene Mason

Darlene Mason

Direct Approach Letter For A Referral Interview

Sara Smith
8 Dunwody Ct.
Savannah, GA 56231

July 29, _____

Mr. James Knox
Vice President of Operations
First Georgia
8621 Sequoia St.
Atlanta, GA 56430

Dear Mr. Knox:

I am writing to you because I have long admired the vision of your company in the marketplace. As Vice President of Operations, your leadership is key to the continued growth and success of your organization.

I am presently looking to expand my career opportunities through the utilization of my skills in project management and line operations. I have over fifteen years of experience in the financial services industry, and now seek a return to my banking roots. With a background in financial analysis, direct and indirect lending, credit, and collections, I have a solid foundation to expand upon.

Please understand, Mr. Knox, I am not applying for a specific position with your company, nor do I expect you do know of any current job openings. What I seek is information to decide if my skills and expertise would fit an organization like your company in Georgia.

When we talk you may have suggestions about which banking divisions can offer interesting, challenging, and rewarding career opportunities. I understand that you have a busy schedule. I can assure you that I will require only ten to fifteen minutes of your time.

Again, I am not asking for a job, I am merely seeking advice and information that will help me decide where I should direct my efforts within the banking industry. I will call your office within the next few days to schedule a meeting time that is convenient for you. Thank you.

Sincerely,

Sara Smith

Sara Smith

Direct Approach Letter For Referral Interview

Michael E. Kingston

126 Gardeners Way, Raleigh, NC 53627   Phone and fax: 404-555-1212

Carter and Kauffman, Inc.
547 Sycamore Lane
Durham, NC 59382

December 2, _____

Dear Mr. Martin:

As a former executive, shareholder and General Counsel of Leman Brothers, a $120 million specialty printing company sold earlier this year, I am now actively seeking a new job opportunity in the Raleigh-Durham area. I believe that, because of my background, I could add significant value to a business in your industry. I would like to meet with you at your convenience to discuss the possibilities and to hear your personal insights and advice.

I earned a Bachelor of Mechanical Engineering from Chapel Hill and an MBA and JD from the University of North Carolina. After 8 years in the private practice of law, I began with Dittler Brothers as Legal and Administrative Director and advanced first to General Counsel and then to expanded duties beyond the traditional lawyer role. In my 15 years at Leman Brothers, I supervised not only the legal department but also the environmental compliance and quality improvement programs, while contributing to strategic planning, risk management, merger/acquisition and strategic partnership programs. I also worked closely with sales, marketing, human relations, security, internal audit, investor relations and public affairs efforts. Enclosed is my resume, with more detailed descriptions of my qualifications.

Please understand that I do not expect your company to have an open position for me at this time, but I believe it would be beneficial to meet with you to learn more about your organization and where and to what extent my capabilities could be of value in the future.

I will call your office on Monday afternoon, December 7, to arrange an appointment. I look forward to meeting you.

Very truly yours,

Michael E. Kingston

Michael E. Kingston

Direct Approach Letter For Referral Interview

222 Westgate Road
Atlanta, GA 35555
March 17, _____

Ms. Rachel Gordon
Chief Executive Officer
Robin Bright Corporation
3562 Orson Rd.
Montgomery, AL 20503

Dear Ms. Gordon:

In reviewing the top ranked manufacturing firms in middle Alabama, I identified Robin Bright as a firm that could be in need of a seasoned industrial manager. I know your status as the industry leader is constantly challenged to improve. I would like to schedule a short meeting in the near future to discuss how my experience may be of value in helping you grow your market share in today's competitive environment.

I began my career in industrial operations as a tool and die maker while studying for my B.S. in Industrial Education from Illinois State University and later earned my M.A. in Business management from Ohio State University. After college, I spent nearly 22 years in the US Army. For the past year, I have been managing the business development efforts of the modern Computer Corporation's Macmillan Richards office. I am responsible for bid proposal development and selling, engineering, logistics and manufacturing environments of workforces as large as 1200 military and 1800 civilians technicians. In my last assignment at the Macmillan Richards Air Logistics Center I guided the sheer metal and machine manufacturing plant services and engineering operations supporting the Depot. In addition, I have led large supply chain management, transportation, and purchasing functions as well as managed the financial and overhead, environmental and safety functions required to ensure success. My people oriented leadership style helped one of my organizations achieve recognition as the Best in the Army. A more detailed summary of my accomplishments is enclosed for your review.

Mr. Gordon, please understand I do not necessarily expect your firm to have an open position, but I do think it would be of value to meet, learn more about your organization and determine if my skills could be of value in the future.

I realize you have a demanding schedule, so I will contact your office next week to arrange an appropriate date for our meeting. Thank you, I look forward to meeting with you.

Sincerely,

Wendell Jenks

Wendell Jenks

Direct Approach Letter For Referral Interview

Steven Collamore
573 Crest Avenue
Longmeadow, MA 01106

February 28th, _____

Mr. Wayne Berry
Miami Communications
45 Ocean Drive
Miami, FL 30001

Dear Mr. Berry:

Recently for family reasons I decided to return to the USA after almost 8 years living and working overseas. I am seeking a new opportunity within the Boston market. As might be expected, I am seeking the help of other Telecom professionals to discuss my current plans, and to seek advice regarding companies in the Boston market that might benefit from my experience in building communications networks.

My background includes 15 years experience with some of the world leaders in the global telecommunications industry. I have held a number of senior management positions on the major projects where my company designed and built state-of-the art communication networks for governments and large nationalized corporations, both domestically and overseas. I have held key roles in functions including project management, contract management, engineering, and business management. I have also been heavily involved in planning and winning new business.

One of the skills that may be of interest to your company is my experience in the planning, building of teams and execution of projects using a high tech workforce. I also have significant experience managing customer satisfaction at the highest levels of the organization, and possess demonstrative negotiation skills. A more detailed summary of some of my major skills and career accomplishments is enclosed for your review.

Mr. Berry, please understand I do not necessarily expect your firm to have an open position but I definitely think it would be of value to learn more about your company and organization, to determine if my skills could be of value in the future.

I know your time is valuable. I will contact you to arrange a brief meeting at a mutually convenient time. I look forward to meeting you.

Sincerely,

Steven Collamore

Steven Collamore

Direct Approach Letter For Referral Interview

Mark V. Reynolds
8645 Samuel Clemens Dr.
Cleveland, OH 45504
info@anywhere.com
(513) 555-1212

May 11, _____

Mrs. Jane Robinson-Mitchell
Manager, Sales HR and Development
Global Airlines International
Mutual Life Building East Tower,
Suite 1200, 3520 Blake St., West
Cleveland, Ohio 45505

Dear Jane:

When I first wrote to you on February 26th, I explained that I was in the initial stages of my job search and I was really gathering information to assist me in coming to an informed decision about potential long-term career options.

Over the course of the past months, I have been able to meet with several people who have provided an enormous amount of data. Having now assessed this research in conjunction with a critical review of my own preferences, I firmly believe my background and credentials would prove to be valuable assets to your team and while I appreciate you may not have any specific openings at the present time, I expect that you are constantly alert to candidates who could fulfill future requirements.

While the attached Statement of Capabilities captures my skills and abilities, I have always believed that personality and a proper "fit" with an employer play a major part in the selection process. As such, I would welcome the opportunity to meet with you for a short period of time to allow you to develop some personal opinions, while presenting any questions related to my past experience and future aspirations.

I will be in touch with you by phone during the week of May 18th and I look forward to speaking with you in the not too distant future.

Sincerely,

Mark V. Reynolds

Mark V. Reynolds

Direct Approach Letter For Referral Interview

Allan Resources

21 W. Fairview, Detroit, MI 45556, Tel. 777-777-7777

September 5, _____

Mr. Peter Olson
546 Cowslip St.
Grande Fork, OR 56321

Dear Mr. Olson:

By form of this letter allow me to introduce myself. I am David Farrell and am the owner of Security Resources. I have been referred to you by an associate of yours, Mark Dayson. I am seeking input and opinions as to the validity of a business concept I am introducing into the local market.

As you can tell from my letterhead, one of the services I offer is Construction Management. I have enclosed a copy of my professional profile for your review, but one of the positions I held for several years was that of a Project Manager with a Design/Build Architectural Firm in my home state of Kentucky. I feel the concept of Construction Management is not well received in the local community. Consequently, there is an opportunity to market this concept well and capture a portion of the market that is currently being served by other building methods.

In addition to "Construction Management" services, I am also offering general "Project Administration" services. These services come in a variety of formats ranging from the tracking of Change Orders, the establishing and conducting of Job Conferences, to offering a modified form of Project Supervision that can be tailored to the needs of a specific budget, project or client.

I also have the need to broker the services of other construction professionals to meet the needs of my clients.

These are a few of the things I would like to talk to you about. Towards that end, I will be contacting you in the next week to set up a meeting of mutual convenience. I know time is valuable, so let me assure you that I will come prepared and keep our meeting brief. As mentioned, I have enclosed a copy of my Professional Profile to assist you in formulating ideas ahead of our meeting. Please feel free to contact me at the numbers contained herein to discuss any questions you may have.

Sincerely,

David Farrell

David Farrell

Enclosure

Referral Approach Letter

5621 Delmar Street
Ruskville, IN 45302

June 2, _____

Ms. Roberta Chokdi
Director of Marketing
Shakespeare-on-the-Green, Inc.
952 E. 6th Street
Indianapolis, IN 45312

Dear Ms. Chokdi:

Mr. Dave Smith, Vice President of Uripophea International, spoke very highly of your experience in Marketing Management and suggested you might be a valuable source of information.

At the present time I am actively seeking a position in marketing research. The enclosed resume outlines my objective and supports it with some of my qualifications and achievements.

Please understand, *I do not expect you to have or know of any current openings.* However, I would appreciate a discussion to seek your ideas, suggestions, comments, and reactions on how I might achieve my objective.

Appreciating your time is valuable, I assure you I will keep our meeting brief. I will call you on Thursday, June 6, to arrange an appointment.

Sincerely,

Lynn Marlow

Lynn Marlow

Enclosure

Thank-You Letter For A Referral Interview

7324 Oak Post Road
Apt. 253
Grand Rapids, MI 54321

April 20, _____

Ms. Jane Peterson
Attorney-at-Law
P. O. Box 5432
Grand Rapids, MI 54322

Dear Ms. Peterson:

Just a brief note to say "thank you" for giving up some of your valuable time to meet with me yesterday.

Your suggestion that I might be well suited for a position with Datawind Software or a similar organization as a troubleshooter was very helpful. I will be contacting Mr. Pete Squire of Datawind to schedule a meeting for further information within the next few days. I very much appreciate this referral.

Again, thank you for your time and assistance, Ms. Peterson. If you happen to think of additional advice or suggestions that may be of assistance in my career search, please call or write me. I'll keep you informed of my progress.

Sincerely,

Julie Rogers

Julie Rogers

Thank-You Letter For A Referral Interview

8324 Corvallis Road
Potomac, MD 20451

October 12, _____

Mr. Rudy King
Operations Manager
Benton Unplugged
5432 18th Street, Ste. 210
Washington, DC 20036

Dear Mr. King:

Thank you again for the opportunity to meet with you.

Your comments and suggestions were very much appreciated. I especially like your idea regarding the impact of time and demographics on the catalogue industry. I certainly agree that the catalogue industry is growing dramatically and could afford some unique opportunities, particularly in the area of CD technology, and I intend to act upon it.

As you suggested, I will be contacting both Lisa Fontaine and Wally Hicks in the near future.

Again, thank you and I will keep you informed of my progress.

Sincerely,

Suzanne Hart

Suzanne Hart

"T" Letter: Responding To A Classified Ad

Gloria Martin
gmart362@anywhere.net

128 Forester Way
Misquamicut, RI 32615
(615) 555-1212 (phone and fax)

April 8, _____

Whitmore Industries
6532 Center Street
Providence, RI 32600

Dear Hiring Manager:

With my background in OD and Training, I bring the skills you need to fill the position for an "Organizational Development and Training Specialist" which appeared in the *Weekly Journal*, dated July 19.

ADVERTISED REQUIREMENTS	MY QUALIFICATIONS
Coordinate all employee development and training needs, evaluating organizational training needs	Proven track record in developing corporate training strategy and programs for 21 site company.
Preparing and /or conducting training programs	Broad developmental expertise in training programs ranging from technology specific to management oriented topics.
Recommending operational training classes and seminars	Strong background in analysis of available resources and determination of best use options.
Evaluating progress of employees	Designed and implemented competency based training programs; designed performance appraisal systems.
Lead facilitator for implementation of employee involvement and empowerment programs	Extensive experience with facilitating team building and empowerment in a variety of cultures ranging from healthcare to public education.
Other OD functions	Diverse experience in analyzing organizations and re-focusing to implement OD programs.

Bachelor's degree in related discipline	MBA with emphasis on organizational studies and human resources.
At least 3 years of experience in training and organizational development	Over 5 years experience in design and implementation of team building, change management and training programs.
Flexible and highly motivated specialist with proven facilitator skills	Diverse experience demonstrates flexibility with emphasis in the OD and training fields as well as demonstrated track record as a facilitator.

It appears that there is a strong match between your requirements and my qualifications. I would like to meet you at your earliest convenience to discuss this opportunity and will be glad to discuss salary requirements during the interview. My resume is enclosed for your further consideration.

Sincerely,

Gloria Martin

Gloria Martin

"T" Letter: Following A Referral Letter

Allan Resources

21 W. Fairview, Detroit, MI 45556, Tel. 777-777-7777

September 12, ———

Mr. Terry Wall
Sterling Group
8321 Center Drive
Detroit, MI 45555

VIA FAX

Dear Mr. Wall:

I want to thank you for the time you spent with me last Friday
discussing your view of the Sterling market as well as the needs
of your organization. I feel there is a degree of mutual benefit
in a relationship between our companies. It was pleasing to hear
of your pledge to quality services and the need for character
based service. It is fair to say we have experienced some of the
same frustrations in our dealing with others in the local develop-
ment/construction community.

Allow me to provide a summary of potential services I could provide based upon what I understand your needs to be.

Your Needs	My Abilities/The Solution
Greater assurance that you are receiving value oriented services in terms of cost, scheduling and measure of quality.	I can provide a consulting service that will confirm the quality of the services you are receiving based upon industry standards, assuring maximum value for your construction dollar.
Quickly and efficiently compose preliminary budget estimates.	I can quickly and efficiently arrive at all levels of preliminary budgeting, as you referred to as phases, in a way that will either sustain or replace the budgets developed by others.
Turnkey administration/coordination of smaller projects.	I can provide a service that will comprehensively manage projects of lesser scope and dollar value, giving you greater control and cost efficiency.

Intelligent liaison within the Construction Community.

I can attend on your behalf all construction oriented meetings and offer a service that would represent and protect your best interests.

I would appreciate an appointment to futher discuss how I could best meet your needs. I'll call you next Thursday to answer any questions you may have concerning my capabilities.

Sincerely,

Jeff Allan

Jeff Allan

"T" Letter: Responding To Classified Ad

David Lee
722 West Chester Avenue
West Chester, MD 26262
410-555-5555

August 3, _____

Box 8201
Baltimore Sun
2290 Main Street
Baltimore, MD 25555

Subject: Application for Vice President of Administration

I am responding to your ad soliciting resumes for the "Vice President of Administration" position which appeared in the *Baltimore Sun*. Having been a business owner, I know the importance of finding a qualified, energetic, customer-focused individual. With my background, I know I am very qualified.

Advertised Requirements	My Qualifications
• Highly Talented	• Have extensive background in administration, having successfully started and operated diverse businesses.
	• BA in business management and economics and minor in accounting.
• Highly customer service oriented	• Achieved business success through effective customer service.
	• Effective in building relationships, solving customer problems and creating win-win situations.
	• Extensive experience to develop and expand loyal customer base to build business and increase profits.
• Energetic	• Positive, can-do attitude.
	• Enjoys new challenges.
• Administration	• Builds a team to accomplish the goals.
	• Proven track record of dealing with details and doing multiple projects on deadlines.

It appears that there is a strong match between your requirements and my qualifications. I would like to meet with you at your earliest convenience to discuss this opportunity. My resume is enclosed for your further consideration.

Sincerely,

David Lee

David Lee

Enclosure

"T" Letter: Responding To A Classified Ad

LARRY JUNO
8069 Brick Street SW
Macon, GA 56431
(425) 555-1212
January 8, _____

Robert Cuchs
Club Management, Inc.
5460 Oleon Rd., Ste. 560
Atlanta, GA 56432

Dear Mr. Cuchs:

In response to your listing, "management opportunity within the OPC/GVAA", for a General Manager, Stovington Golf and Country Club, Macon, Georgia, please consider the following:

YOUR REQUIREMENTS	MY QUALIFICATIONS
Previous experience as a G/M desired, and a college degree preferred	Just completed assignment as General Manager of a 350 member private country club; BA degree from The University of Georgia.
Demonstrated strengths in accounting; team building and delivering on expectations	Over ten years experience in accounting and team building, personal and professional references verify I exceeded Membership/ Board expectations.
Experience in budgeting and financial management, including capital expenditure forecasting and strategic planning	Over eight years experience producing consistent revenue streams while controlling expenses. Generated positive cash flow for capital improvement funding. Budgeted for/ controlled capital expenditures averaging $75,000 annually.
Experience in planning, organizing, and supervising banquets and parties	Planned, organized, and supervised events from casual to elegant formal 5-course dining affairs for up to 800 guests.
Superior food operations background	Hands on food operations experience plus formal schooling in a la carte food, beverage, and wine. Served on Corporation of National Food and Beverage Committee.
Will have overall knowledge of club operations to include golf shop operations, course maintenance, community/board relations skills, and use of computers	Have first hand working knowledge of club operations: includes golf course/proshop operations and course maintenance, plus formal instruction provided by DDE. Community relations highlights in Atlanta and Macon. Excellent working knowledge of computers and computer software designed for clubs.

Ability to supervise staff, implement training programs; will possess a hands-on management style as a team builder	Over 15 years experience as supervisor. Hold the designation club Management & Operations Trainer. Practice a hands-on/team building management style.
Must be "visible", with a warm personality that engages and fosters member use of facilities	Professional references will verify "visibility", and interview will confirm personality ideal for the General Manager position.

Enclosed is my resume for consideration.

Sincerely,

Larry Juno

Larry Juno

"T" Letter: Following Referral Interview

Robert Matheson

123 Fromish Blvd.
Toronto, Ontario M6T 3K8
Canada

Fax 416-555-5555
Home Phone 416-444-4444
Email: robert@anywhere.net

Friday, March 5, _____

Sharpsters Canada, Inc.
156 Whetstone Lane
Toronto, Ontario
M6R 2L4

Attn: Peter Sackey

Dear Mr. Sackey:

Thank you very much for taking as much time as you did to talk with me last Tuesday. I have been reflecting on our conversation and the information we shared. I have drafted below, my understanding of the kind of individual you indicated you needed to add to your team. I also felt it would be beneficial to you if I summarize the skills I have that would benefit Sharpsters Canada Inc.

I realize this position may still be evolving, but I am very excited at the opportunities I see where I can make an immediate impact with Sharpsters. I believe my background would enable me to recommend immediate strategies in planning and executing sales programs and building long term relationships with National Accounts which be both cost effective and profitable.

I have considered your comments and observations regarding the requirements you feel you need. To assist you in becoming confident as I am that I can satisfy your requirements, I have included my qualifications.

Your Requirements	My Qualifications
An individual with existing relationships with national accounts and distributors throughout Canada.	Recognized expertise in the seasonal lawn and garden market with over 10 years experience. Established working relationships with key national accounts such as Super Value, Conner Canada, Total Hardware as well as regional distributors such as Scotia Seed, Greenthumb, Rory's, Easton, and Milli's.

Organizational skills to deliver programs to key accounts in a timely manner.	Experienced in developing and communicating marketing plans to accounts across Canada in a timely and efficient manner maximizing available resources and profitability. Proficiency in maximizing sales coverage on a national basis with minimal expense.
Superior communication skills.	Exceptional communicator as demonstrated by numerous presentations to clients, educational groups and special interest groups. Able to uncover and appeal to customer needs by questioning, listening and presenting favorably received recommendations.
Ability to blend sales programs of various product lines under one brand.	Demonstrated ability to develop strategies and programs to market products under a single brand strategy, allowing customers a diverse selection of products and maximizing sales to customers.
Expand existing market.	Worked with existing customers to develop new sales strategies increasing sales and profitability for both the customer and the company.
Knowledge of how national accounts work in the seasonal market.	Demonstrated ability and proficiency in working with national accounts from late spring Line Reviews through mid summer presentations, trade shows, etc. Developed marketing strategies with individual accounts while maximizing corporate profitability.
Creative thinker.	Initiated new product development designed to capitalize on specialty markets. Established packaging requirements, pricing thresholds and sales criteria increasing average sales and profitability by as much as 20% per customer.

Simon, thank you very much for the time you spent with me and the information you shared. As you requested, I am also including a copy of my references with this letter for your review. I would like to contact you late next week to discuss your thoughts on my enclosed perceptions of your needs I look forward to speaking with you again soon

Sincerely,

Robert Matheson

Robert Matheson

Thank-You Letter: Following Interview

Arthur Bondoin
543 Winchester Way
Falls Church, VA 22105
703/555-1212

November 23, _____

Frank Furley
Sun Signal Friction Works
4368 Malney Road
Fairfax, VA 22185

Dear Frank:

Thank you very much for taking time to meet with me on Thursday, February 4th to discuss the HS&E Manager position at Sun Signal Friction Works. It is evident from our conversation, this is a great opportunity and I am looking forward to the next step in the process.

The issues you spoke of were challenging and I believe I can address them for you in short order:

1) You have focused on reducing the frequency and number of injuries at the Plant and the time has come to bring an HS&E, professional into your leadership team.

   I have nearly 15 years of successful HS&E compliance and management experience. Recently, acting as the HS&E Manager for a plant, the facility was able to reduce recordable injuries by over 66% in two years. Over the last five years I have served on several key leadership teams throughout Fuelco and I take great enjoyment in being part of a tightly knit team.

2) You have a few internal audit findings to resolve.

   Having been both an auditor and on the receiving end of many HS&E audits performed by Corporate and State and Federal regulators, I am confident we can address the current issues and put action plans in place in order to ensure proper preparation for any future audits. This could be our first priority!!

3) Lastly, you mentioned, with a small leadership team and limited resources, you all must wear many "hats."

   I look forward to utilizing my experience in developing business plans and strategies as a part of your team. In addition to other varied duties, I can see us growing the business, capturing more of the light truck market and improving profitability.

As you can tell, I am extremely interested in joining the Sun Signal Friction Works group and I will call to touch base on your progress if you don't have the opportunity to contact me in the very near future. Again, thank you for the opportunity to speak with you and your team.

Sincerely,

Arthur Bondoin

Arthur Bondoin

General Cover Letter To Recruiters

366 East Third Street
Columbia, MO 36251

August 3, _____

Mr. Jerry Simpson
President
Simpson & Associates
9400 Marlboro Street
Columbia, MO 36252

Dear Mr. Simpson:

After spending the last 10 years as President and CEO of Venus Products International, I am anxious to tackle new challenges. As an impact player who has had a history of dramatic achievements at every level, I look forward to working with you and your staff in my career pursuits.

Below is a brief listing of items of interest.

Objective:	CEO or Senior Level Position in Sales.
Background:	Thorough understanding and first hand experience in managing Sales and Marketing functions.
Industry:	Extensive experience in the marine and HVAC industries; anxious to explore other options as well.
Highlights:	Turned around 5 companies, achieving double digit sales growth and a 20% ROI. Led Sales and Marketing functions to unprecedented levels of success. Recognized by HVAC national membership as Woman of the Year.
Salary Expectations:	$125K - $175K plus incentives, depending upon the the overall package and level of challenge.
Geographical Preference:	Open to relocation, willing to travel.

Enclosed is a resume which lists other achievements and provides an overview of my career.

If you should desire any further information, please contact me at (562) 555-1212. I look forward to hearing from you.

Sincerely,

Shawna Leviston

Shawna Leviston

Enclosure

Response To A Blind Advertisement

6666 Adkins Lane
Holyoke, MA 01180

June 10, _____

Business Daily
c/o The Journal Newspapers
1805 Quark Road
Hartford, CT 12365

Dear Advertiser:

In response to your advertisement dated June 8, 1997, in the <u>National Daily</u> for "Vice President of Manufacturing," please consider the following:

<u>Your Requirements</u>	<u>My Qualifications</u>
Set and make happen aggressive monthly shipping plan	Over 8 years aggressive direct sales program/production management experience; PLANNED, SCHEDULED, COORDINATED, EXPEDITED 100+ electronic defense contracts, meeting monthly fab, test, Q.C. shipping schedules to include stateside/offshore subcontracting.
Bring continuous stream of new products from engineering release to production inventory ready to ship	Over 8 years of aggressive COORDINATED/INTEGRATED engineering configuration manufacturing new/prototype and existing designs from release to production—stock—delivery in multi-project environment.
Plan and implement a cost reduction program that has major influence on the company's performance	IMPLEMENTED/MONITORED earned value system; recovered $1M loss; INITIATED economies-of-scale production; increased 2% loss to 10% profit for business segment.
Maintain the company's reputation for providing quality products	INTEGRATED/MONITORED engineering, manufacturing, quality activities; CONDUCTED CCB reviews; won follow-on contracts.

Enclosed is my resume for your consideration.

Sincerely,

Jennifer Adams

Jennifer Adams

Enclosure

Cover Letter For A Focus Piece

732 Braewood Lane
Wilmington, Delaware 36204

February 12, _____

Mr. Duncan Wire
President
Pure Sight Co.
326 Clearview Road
Wilmington, DE 36254

Dear Mr. Wire:

I have been going over in my mind the insights that both you and Rex provided to me when we met a week ago Thursday. You were very gracious and I truly would enjoy working with you.

I have developed some perceptions about your current needs, as well as my capability to make a positive contribution.

This comparison is shown in the enclosed "Focus Piece." I would like to have another brief meeting with you for the purpose of you validating my perceptions. I know you are extremely busy right now so I'll call you on Monday, February 20, to arrange a time that is convenient for you.

Sincerely,

Randy Doogan

Randy Doogan

Enclosure

Cover Letter

Sid Fontaine
P.O. Box 5632
398 Wayfield Way
Mt. Aerie, MD 20741
(410) 555-1212

Mike Fletcher
TRM Recruiting
983 Paradise St.
Frederick, MD 20743

October 6, _____

Dear Mr. Fletcher:

Subject: Plant and Production Management and/or Operations Management Position

Your organization was referred to me as one that may have an interest in reviewing my credentials for one of your client assignments.

I am a manufacturing and production manager with 12 years experience in plant management and plant operations. I have proven expertise in manpower and materials planning, inventory and quality control, safety and sanitation, and production; and competence in managing, directing, and developing people in union and non-union environments. I am seeking a position in plant and production management and/or operations management in the Mid-Atlantic area.

Your consideration is greatly appreciated. I would be pleased to discuss with you in further detail specific elements of my background, qualifications, and future interest with respect to your client requirements.

Sincerely,

Sid Fontaine

Sid Fontaine

Enclosure: Resume

Referral Approach Letter

563 Humber Avenue
Milton
Ontario C5S 3R6
Tel: (905) 555-5555
Fax: (905) 444-4444
e-mail: info@anywhere.net

Ms. Sharon Masterson
Complete Media Inc.
354 Queen Street East, Suite 204
Milton
Ontario L6T 3M8

6th December _____

Dear Sharon:

I believe that my good friend, George Collins, has been in touch with you on my behalf. As you know, I have recently left the U.K. and settled here in Milton.

With nearly 20 years experience in cinema distribution and related media environments, I am actively considering my next career step in line with long-range objectives. The enclosed resume outlines my objective and supports it with details of my background and achievements. My specific interests lie in the area of marketing and promotion or project development.

Please understand that I'm not expecting you to have a job at Rhombus or even to know of one elsewhere. Instead, as I'm new to Milton, I am seeking your advice and insight with regard to how I could progress and would appreciate a discussion to seek your input and comments.

I appreciate that your time is valuable and I assure you that I will keep our meeting brief. I'll call you towards the end of next week (week commencing Monday, 9th December) in order to arrange an appointment.

Best Wishes,

Wendell MacBride

Wendell MacBride

Focus Piece
(As Part of a Letter)

599 Beach Road
Weekapaug, RI 26321
April 5, _____

Peter Davis, President
Ultra Link Inc.
256 Mooring Way
Mystic, CT 56432

Dear Mr. Davis:

Since our last conversation on Thursday, March 13, I have been reflecting over the information we exchanged and felt it might be beneficial to you if I summarized the strong administrative and technical skills I could bring to the position of Manager of Engineering Services.

I realize this position may still be evolving, but I am still very excited about the opportunities I see where I can have an immediate impact in this area. I feel my background would enable me to recommend methodologies, planning strategies, procedures and services which would be cost effective and would also generate new revenue.

I have tried to consider the input and information I have received from all areas of your organization regarding the emphasis of this position, and have listed these areas below. To assist you in becoming as confident as I am that I can satisfy all your needs in this position, I have also included my qualifications.

Your Requirements	My Qualifications
Develop new services from existing system capabilities	Planned and directed consultation and support to customers; assisting them in testing, evaluating, and using of new systems. Trained customer and sub-contractor during installation of $150MM prototype system resulting in an additional 47 sites.
Assist Engineering and network operations in setting, new procedures, training, systems development, and unique department projects	Developed and administered a quality program which included teamwork and procedures used (by a staff of 150) during design, testing, evaluation, training, and support of new systems. This became the company criterion for numerous other unique projects valued at over $100MM each.
Provide sales support to corporate clients	Provided consultation and sales support to new and existing sites, and served as corporate liaison for planning and installation of a $6MM multi-location system (included suggestive selling of additional $300K in accessories).
Direct preparation of expansion plans and budget documents	Planned, forecasted, and managed staff budgets successfully for 10 years; scheduled and tracked all task elements of systems; and verified system compatibility and performance. Directed and managed the system test effort (with a staff of 20) which resulted in detecting a performance overload, immediately saving a $9MM sale and eliminating complaints and lost revenue from over 400 customer sites.

Expand marketing plans into system expansion and design requirements	Worked with customer, design, and requirement groups to assure needs of all groups were met for new products. Identified and resolved a design flow which would have failed for the first $6MM unit and jeopardized 1000 additional units, allowing generation of annual sales of $400MM.
Develop strong, relations with industry and vendors	Recognized expertise: over 15 years experience as vendors liaison between customers, engineering, and manufacturing to create a new telecommunications choke system that generated $700K additional revenue.
Develop and promote new products and markets	Planned, budgeted, staffed, implemented, and evaluated new and prototype systems. Corrected a 6 month out-of line schedule for a prototype system salvaging a $40MM sale.
Define customer feature and service requirements	Consulted with and supported customer requirements for over 12 years. Planned and over-saw the procedures and evaluation techniques used by over 1000 customers to evaluate products and services with annual sales volume over $400MM.
Monitor and assess new techniques	Planned, budgeted, staffed, and developed facilities to evaluate new technologies. Planned, constructed, and integrated hardware, software, and networking for new and existing laboratories costing over $60MM. Provided direction and leadership for a staff of 20 during product evaluation.
Develop product compatibility standards	Determined new product compatibility, user friendliness, performance, and documentation accuracy. Directed system test effort (staff of 20), and made recommendations that resulted in resolution of a network performance overload saving a $9MM sale and complaints from 400 sites.

Regarding my experience, please note I have been especially effective in the areas of service to the customer and engineering, as well as planning, administration, new product evaluation, and revenue generation.

I am very interested in learning more about your needs in this area and in further discussing with you how my abilities and experience can significantly impact the needs of your organization. I am very excited about the possibility of joining your dynamic organization and will call you Thursday, April 8, to determine the next step.

Sincerely,

Abigail Page

Abigail Page

Follow-up Letter with Focus Piece

Ronald Feicht

653 German Way • Big Sky, Wyoming 84628 • 919/555-1212 • ron@anywhere.net

Ms. Sara Wong
Materials and Logistics Manager
Construction Realty
PO Box 333
Nuevo, WY 84623

Dear Sara:

Thank you for taking the time to speak with me last Friday morning the 20th of March. I really enjoyed meeting you and agree with your point of view on what responsibilities a scheduler position should involve. I am taking this opportunity to write to you with the thought that I may help you in the very difficult process you face in narrowing down the good many candidates who have responded to the advertisement to those few exceptional ones that you have interviewed and may be in the final selection process.

After discussing your perception on the problems you see as obstacles for success at Construction Realty, I have attached a "focus piece" to elaborate on those needs and the aspects of my background and experience I feel will meet those needs.

I would like to discuss the attached "focus piece" at your convenience. I feel confident my experience in scheduling and production planning, along with extensive interaction with both customers and production workers, will be a profitable and effective augmentation to your team. Thank you again for the consideration.

Sincerely,

Ronald Feicht

Ronald Feicht

Ronald Feicht

653 German Way • Big Sky, Wyoming 84628 • 919/555-1212 • ron@anywhere.net

Focus Piece

Construction Realty
Materials and Logistic Management

Construction Realty

1. Construction Realty understands that the usage of a cardex manual inventory system is antiquated, slow, subject to loss of the cards and very inefficent. To achieve the goals of higher customer satisfaction and profitability, it must rely on experienced and motivated professionals, with the latest tools to keep the inventory current and the costs down.

    With a proven track record in inventory planning and scheduling of thousands of part numbers for manufacturing, I have been successful in working through the transition from a manual to automated systems for existing plants and those in a start up mode.

2. The Materials and Logistics group is responsible for the **production line stability at all times,** and must be able to react to line changes, customer needs, design changes, and must maintain daily contact with management and customers to ensure the continued growth and success of the company.

    I have the experience of working with a mixed line set up, both as a planner/scheduler as well as a line supervisor and can provide information and training to reducing the down time involved with changes in production requirements.

3 . Teamwork is the key to making sure all persons within the organization share the same vision for success that is required for Construction Realty to succeed in the global marketplace.

    With a proven track record in creating and maintaining a highly efficient and motivated team that clearly understands it's objectives and is committed to exceeding it's goals, I have been successful mainly by creating an environment that stresses creativity, initiative, accountability, and teamwork.

I am also continually committed to enhancing my knowledge and understanding of the new tools, techniques, and methodologies emerging in the manufacturing and production control industry that will help establish a new and very successful Master Production Scheduler position at Construction Realty. Furthermore, I am still a participating member of the local APICS chapter, which I helped restart and was the president for two years upon rebirth of the dormant chapter.

Follow-up Letter With Focus Piece

543 Southern Lane
Gainesville, FL 64321

September 5, _____

Peter Fontaine
Rush Services, Inc.
25 Counter Way
Gainesville, FL 64322

Dear Peter:

Thank you for taking time out of your busy schedule to allow me the opportunity to speak with you concerning my career change in July. I am taking this opportunity to write you with the thought that I may offer some information relative to the three major challenges you mentioned during our discussion.

As previously discussed, I would be keeping you informed as to my career change progress. This letter is being sent as a follow-up to get your feedback on my approach.

I have been going over in my mind the insights and expectations you provided to me when we talked in July. You were very helpful and I truly appreciated your comments. I have listed some of the current needs you mentioned, as well as my capability to make a positive contribution.

This comparison is shown in the enclosed "Focus Piece."

I will call you the week of September 14 to follow-up on my comments.

Sincerely,

Seth Gordon

Seth Gordon

Enclosure

Rush Services, Inc.
Focus Piece

1.   Rush Services, Inc. requires a "sense of urgency" to meet the high speed
      manufacturing needs.

*My varied experience in manufacturing has provided many opportunities to review
and evaluate situations which required quick improvements. The following are but
two examples:*
*...initiated cost control measures by evaluating past methods and developing a
"cost containment" plan. The result was a **$2 million below budget performance
within 9 months.***
*...spearheaded reorganization and directed improvement program for plant
bottleneck operation. Result was a **15% decrease in equipment downtime within 6
months.** Operation achieved record uptime levels.*

2.   Rush Services, Inc. seeks experience transferable to their product.

*Having successfully held 2 varied positions and made 5 relocation transfers, my
managerial skills have enabled me to:*
*...utilize team development skills focused in motivational techniques based on
organizational improvement, goal establishment and revitalized proficiency training programs for our facility to set 12 records in output, waste, energy, and atten-
dance management in 20 months. By accomplishing these records, the production
organization impacted the bottom line profitability by $1.2 million. **I believe I can
accomplish similar results for any product line.***

3.   Current union-employer relations are good. Rush Services, Inc. requires manage-
      ment philosophies in keeping with current atmosphere.

*My prior manufacturing management experiences have allowed me the opportu-
nity to work with 4 different local union organizations and a large number of
union representatives with good success. An example of one of our cooperative
efforts was to be the first Business Center at the Macmillan facility to develop
monthly union-management team meetings with all floor managers and stewards to
discuss contractual and other more general concerns. Eventually ALL of the other
Business Centers followed our lead and established their own meetings.*

I am continually committed to enhancing my knowledge and understanding of the new
tools, techniques and methodologies emerging in manufacturing management to help establish successful improvements in production, profits and employee relations. Furthermore, I am extensively involved in expanding my financial expertise through seminars,
classes, and practical applications, which I believe allows me to make continuing financial
improvements in any positions I hold.

Follow-Up Letter With Attachment

Juan Petrez
8625 Gelia Road
Houston, TX 65432

May 27, _____

Barry Anderson
CEO
Life Homes, Inc.
5643 Runningdale St.
Houston, TX 65431

Dear Mr. Anderson:

I really enjoyed our meeting last week, as well as meeting Pete and Karin yesterday. My discussions with you and your colleagues have intensified my interest in finding a way for us to work together. I believe I will be a valuable addition to your management team. Many of the issues you are facing are similar to situations that I helped solve at Feathers Interactive and Rundale Corporation.

- Pricing strategies for Internet software
- Using customers or alliance partners to distribute products
- Building positive working relationships with investors
- Pursuing capital investment while maintaining control of the organization you built
- Finding funding alternatives from non-traditional sources

I have included an example of a problem I faced at Feathers Interactive, which is similar to problems you may face. In fact, this project required extensive business modeling including a detailed application of funds, projected balance sheets, projected statements of sources and uses of funds.

Again, thank you for the time you took out of your busy schedule to talk with me. After you've had a chance to review the attachment, I'll give you a call to get your reactions.

Sincerely,

Juan Petrez

Juan Petrez

Attachment

Juan Petrez
May 27, 1998
Page 2

ATTACHMENT

PROBLEM

Develop forecasts and projections based on business plans that were constantly changing with the dynamic Internet market. The traditional three month process of writing a business plan and creating the models was and is not appropriate in the ever changing world of the Internet.

STRATEGY

We all had to learn to be flexible and create plans and models that could easily be adapted to a fluid business environment. I utilized my outstanding spreadsheet skills to build models where the variables could easily be changed and documented. The spreadsheets I created were user friendly and could be revised with very little effort. Any changes made to the projections would flow through to the projected income statements, balance sheets, sources and uses of funds.

RESULTS

I created a reliable and transferable business model which could be amended quickly in order to provide the CEO with timely projections assessing the impact of any changes to the business plan. The projected financial statements created by the model were in accordance with GAAP. These easily modified forecasts allowed the management team and investment bankers to quickly provide relevant numbers to prospective strategic partners and investors ultimately resulting in Feathers Interactive's goal, selling the company for over $20 million.

Follow-Up Letter To A Recruiter
(After An Initial Telephone Call)

453 Alden
Rockville, MD 20854

March 19, _____

Mr. Marc Cowen
Executive Vice President
Cowen and Sons
3894 Smucker Road
Bethesda, MD 20851

Dear Mr. Cowen:

Thank you for talking to me today. My resume is enclosed, as you requested. Let me elaborate below on some of the things I have done.

During my tenure with the health planning authorities of Smithton and the North Peoria Health Systems Agency, I reviewed and made recommendations on over $10 million worth of projects which would impact the health and well-being of almost one million people.

I have over ten years experience in policy analysis, planning, and implementation. I have:

- Written a "how to do it" manual for approximately 4,000 physicians which explained how to gain control over local health planning;
- Prepared and published a directory of community-based organizations with over 250 listings of service organizations;
- Advised an HMO on survival strategies in regard to Federal interaction and marketing concepts to increase subscriber enrollments;
- Designed the evaluation methodology used by the National Heart Foundation, Southern Illinois chapter, to evaluate their programming.

I have a Master's Degree in Urban and Regional Planning from University of Northern Illinois and a B.A. in Government and Politics from the University of Chicago.

I would welcome the opportunity to discuss further details of my experience in an interview.

Sincerely,

Diana Melbourne

Diana Melbourne
Enclosure

Thank-You Letter: Following Referral Interview

563 Humber Avenue
Milton
Ontario C5S 3R6
Tel: (905) 555-5555
Fax: (905) 444-4444
e-mail: info@anywhere.net

Ms. Sharon Masterson
Complete Media Inc.
354 Queen Street East, Suite 204
Milton
Ontario L6T 3M8

13th December _____

Dear Sharon:

Thank you again for the opportunity to meet with you yesterday.

Your comments and suggestions were very much appreciated. We spoke briefly about Victor Esta. Enclosed is my copy of the FLAMENCO film that he made a couple of years ago (with Carlos Mariani as DP). I hope you and Dick Steinberg enjoy it. I saw it at the London Film Festival last year and was knocked out by it. Olé!

There's no great hurry to get it back to me; sometime in the New Year will do fine.

Meanwhile, I shall be contacting Mary Smith, Shaun O'Leary, George Peters and probably Carol Masters as you suggest.

Again, thank you enormously for your time and I will keep you informed of my progress!

Best wishes,

Wendell MacBride

Wendell MacBride

APPENDIX

BERNARD HALDANE ASSOCIATES NETWORK

As we noted previously, self-directed career books can help you become more effective with your job search. They outline useful principles, suggest effective strategies, and explain how you and others can achieve your own job and career success. That's our purpose in writing this and other books in the "Haldane's Best" series. We believe you can benefit greatly from the methods we have developed over the years and used successfully with thousands of our clients.

We know the Haldane methods work because our clients are real cases of success that go far beyond the anecdotal. Indeed, our files are filled with unsolicited testimonials from former clients who have shared their insights into what really worked—evidence of our effectiveness in delivering what we promise our clients. We've shared some of these testimonials throughout the text of this book. What especially pleases us as career professionals is the fact that we've helped change the lives of so many people who have gone on to renewed career success. They discovered new opportunities that were a perfect fit for their particular interests, skills, and abilities. By focusing on their strengths and identifying their motivated skills and abilities, they were able to chart new and exciting career directions.

> ### Client Feedback
>
> *"You cannot ask questions of a book. You cannot get feedback on what to do from a book. And most of all, no book can help you with a job hunting campaign designed specifically for you. This is where Haldane comes in."*
>
> —J.A.C.
>
> *"I felt I could read a book or two on resumes and the world would beat a path to my door. What you did was to provide a step-by-step process for developing an effective marketing campaign."*
>
> —W.G.S.

But our clients didn't achieve success overnight nor on their own. They worked with a structure, a schedule, and a vision of what they wanted to do next with their lives. Most important of all, they worked with a Career Advisor who helped them every step of the way. What we and other career specialists have learned over the years is no real secret, but it's worth repeating: most job seekers can benefit tremendously by working with a trained and experienced career professional who helps them complete each step of the career management process.

Our methods are not quick and easy, nor do they come naturally to most people—especially if you want to make the right career move. Many of our clients come to us after several weeks and months of frustrated efforts in conducting their own job search. Some tried doing everything according to the books, but they soon discovered that the books are only as good as the actions and outcomes that follow. What they most needed, and later appreciated, was a career professional whom they could work with in completing the critical assessment work (Success Factor Analysis) and in relating that key data to all other stages in their job search, from resume and letter writing to networking and interviewing. Using the proprietary Career Strategy 2000 electronic system, they gained access to a huge database of opportunities and employers. Once our clients decide to "do it the Haldane way" with a Career Advisor, they get surprising results. Again and again their testimonials emphasize the importance of completing Success Factor Analysis, developing a Haldane objective, networking, writing focused resumes and "T" letters, and interviewing and negotiating salary according to Haldane principles. Most important of all, they point out the value of having someone there—a Haldane Career Advisor—to guide them through the psychological ups and downs that often come with the highly ego-involved and rejection-ridden job finding process.

There's a season for everything, be it reading a self-directed career book or contacting a career professional for assistance. We've shared with you our insights and strategies by writing this book. Now it's up to you to take the next step. What you do next may make a critical difference in your career and your life. You may well discover your dream job on your own because you organized a Haldane-principled job search. If and when you feel you could benefit from the assistance of a career professional, please consider the Haldane network of Career Advisors. They have an exceptional track record of success based upon the methods outlined in this and other books in the "Haldane's Best" series. For your convenience, we've listed, along with contact information, the more than 80 offices that make up the Haldane network in the United States, Canada, and the United Kingdom. You can contact the office nearest you for more information and arrange for a free consultation. Please visit our Web site for additional information on Bernard Haldane Associates:

www.jobhunting.com

Bernard Haldane Associates Offices

United States

ALABAMA:

10 Inverness Parkway, Suite 125
Birmingham, AL 35242
(205) 991-9134; Fax (205) 991-7164
bhaadm@aol.com

4725 Whitesburg Dr.; Suite 202
Huntsville, AL 35801
(256) 880-9500; Fax (256) 880-9522
bhahts@aol.com

ARIZONA:

3101 N. Central Avenue, Suite 1560
Phoenix, AZ 85012
(602) 248-8893; Fax (602) 248-8987
bhaphoenix@aol.com

5151 E. Broadway, Suite 390
Tucson, AZ 85711
(520) 790-2767; Fax (520) 790-2992
bha@azstarnet.com

CALIFORNIA:

1801 Avenue of the Stars, Suite 1011
Los Angeles, CA 90067
(310) 203-0955; Fax (310) 203-0933
careers@haldane.com

8801 Folsom Blvd., Suite 100
Sacramento, CA 95826
(916) 381-5094; Fax (916) 381-6506
haldane@job-hunting.com

8880 Rio San Diego Drive, Suite 300
San Diego, CA 92108
(619) 299-1424; Fax (619) 299-5340
sdbha@yahoo.com

388 Market Street, Suite 1600
San Francisco, CA 94111
(415) 391-8087; Fax (415) 391-4009
haldane@job-hunting.com

181 Metro Drive, Suite 410
San Jose, CA 95110-1346
(408) 437-9200; Fax (408) 437-1300
haldane@job-hunting.com

Pacific Plaza, Suite 220
1340 Treat Blvd.
Walnut Creek, CA 94596
(925) 945-0776; Fax (925) 939-3764
haldane@job-hunting.com

COLORADO:

The Registry, 1113 Spruce Street
Boulder, CO 80302
(303) 571-1757; Fax (303) 825-5900
jobhunt@haldane.com

Plaza of the Rockies,
111 S. Tejon Street, Suite 610
Colorado Springs, CO 80903-2263
(719) 634-8000; Fax (719) 635-8008
jobhunt@haldane.com

1625 Broadway, #2550
Denver, CO 80202
(303) 825-5700; Fax (303) 825-5900
jobhunt@haldane.com

Denver Technological Center
8400 E. Prentice Ave., Suite 301
Englewood, CO 80111
(303) 793-3800, Fax (303) 793-3040
jobhunt@haldane.com

Poudre Valley Center
1075 W. Horsetooth Road, Suite 204
Fort Collins, CO 80526
(970) 223-5459; Fax (970) 226-2757
jobhunt@haldane.com

CONNECTICUT:

State House Square
Six Central Row
Hartford, CT 06103-2701
(860) 247-7500; Fax (860) 247-1213
hartford@haldane.com

FLORIDA:

6622 Southpoint Dr. So., Suite 340
Jacksonville, FL 32216
(904) 296-6802; Fax (904) 296-3506
haldane340@msn.com

901 North Lake Destiny Drive, Suite 379
Maitland, FL 32751 **(Orlando)**
(407) 660-8323; Fax (407) 660-2434
bhaorlando@aol.com

5100 W. Kennedy Blvd., Suite 425
Tampa, FL 33609
(813) 287-1393; Fax (813) 289-4125
haldane@worldnet.att.net

GEORGIA:

4170 Ashford Dunwoody Road, Suite 575
Atlanta, GA 30319
(404) 255-3184; Fax (404) 250-1165
haldane@mindspring.com

ILLINOIS:

One Magnificent Mile
980 N. Michigan Ave., Suite 1400
Chicago, IL 60611
(312) 214-4920; Fax (312) 214-7674
jobs@bhaldane.com

One Tower Lane, Suite 1700
Oakbrook Terrace, IL 60181
(630) 573-2923; Fax (630) 574-7048
jobs@bhaldane.com

1901 N. Roselle Road, Suite 800
Schaumburg, IL 60195
(847) 490-6454; Fax (847) 490-6529
jobs@bhaldane.com

INDIANA:

8888 Keystone Crossing, Suite 1675
Indianapolis, IN 46240
(317) 846-6062; Fax (317) 846-6354
bha_indy_admn@worldnet.att.net

IOWA:

6165 NW 86th Street
Johnston, IA 50131 **(Des Moines)**
(515) 727-1623; Fax (515) 727-1673
jobs@bhaldane.com

KANSAS:

7007 College Blvd., Suite 727
Overland Park, KS 66211
(913) 327-0300; Fax (913) 327-7067
kchaldane@qni.com

2024 N. Woodlawn, Suite 402
Wichita, KS 67208
(316) 687-5333; Fax (316) 689-6924
bhaldane@swbell.net

KENTUCKY:

330 E. Main Street, Suite 200
Lexington, KY 40507
(606) 255-2163; Fax (606) 231-0737
bha_lex_admn@worldnet.att.net

9100 Shelbyville Rd., Suite 280
Louisville, KY 40222
(502) 326-5121; Fax (502) 426-5348
bha_louis_admn@worldnet.att.net

MAINE:

477 Congress Street, 5th Floor
Portland, ME 04101-3406
(207) 772-1700; Fax (207) 772-7117
jobhunting@haldane.com

MASSACHUSETTS:

277 Dartmouth St.
Boston, MA 02116-2800
(617) 247-2500; Fax (617) 247-7171
jobhunting@haldane.com

10 Mechanic Street
Worcester, MA 01608
(508) 767-0100; Fax (508) 767-0300
jobhunting@haldane.com

MICHIGAN:

5777 West Maple Rd., Suite 190
West Bloomfield, MI 48322 **(Detroit)**
(248) 737-4700; Fax (248) 737-4789
bhadet@coast.net

MINNESOTA:

3433 Broadway St., N.E., Suite 440
Minneapolis, MN 55413
(612) 378-0600; Fax (612) 378-9225
jobs@bhaldane.com

MISSOURI:

680 Craig Road, Suite 400
St. Louis, MO 63141
(314) 991-5444; Fax (314) 991-5207
careers@haldanestl.com

NEBRASKA:

12020 Shamrock Plaza, Suite 200
Omaha, NE 68154
(402) 330-9461; Fax (402) 330-9847
omaha@haldanestl.com

NEW HAMPSHIRE:

20 Trafalgar Square, Suite 452
Nashua, NH 03063
(603) 886-4200; Fax (603) 886-4242
jobhunting@haldane.com

NEW JERSEY:

The Atrium, E. 80 Route 4, Suite 110
Paramus, NJ 07652
(201) 587-9898; Fax (201) 587-9119
jobs@bhaldane.com

100 Princeton Overlook Center, Suite 100
Princeton, NJ 08540
(609) 987-0400; Fax (609) 987-0011
jobs@bhaldane.com

NEW YORK:

80 State Street, 11th Floor
Albany, NY 12207

(518) 447-1000; Fax (518) 447-0011
jobhunting@haldane.com

838 Crosskey Office Park
Fairport, NY 14450 **(Rochester)**
(716) 425-0550; Fax (716) 425-0554
haldane@frontiernet.net

261 Madison Avenue, Suite 1504
New York, NY 10016
(212) 490-7799; Fax (212) 490-1712
jobs@bhaldane.com

300 International Drive, Suite 213
Williamsville, NY 14221 **(Buffalo)**
(716) 626-3400; Fax (716) 626-3402
jobhunting@haldane.com

NORTH CAROLINA:

6100 Fairview Road, Suite 355
Charlotte, NC 28210
(704) 643-5959; Fax (704) 556-1674
charlotte@haldanestl.com

4011 West Chase Blvd., Suite 210
Raleigh, NC 27607
(919) 546-9759; Fax (919) 546-9766
raleigh@haldanestl.com

OHIO:

3250 W. Market Street, Suite 307
Akron, OH 44333
(330) 867-7889; Fax (330) 867-7874
gcmg_hq@worldnet.att.net

625 Eden Park Drive, Suite 775
Cincinnati, OH 45202
(513) 621-4440; Fax (513) 562-8943
bha_cincy_admn@worldnet.att.net

6500 Rockside Rd., Suite 180
Cleveland, OH 44131
(216) 447-0166 ; Fax (216) 447-0015
bha_clev_admn@worldnet.att.net

111 West Rich Street, Suite 480
Columbus, OH 43215
(614) 224-2322; Fax (614) 224-2333
bha_colb_admn@worldnet.att.net

Fifth Third Center
110 N. Main Street, Suite 1280
Dayton, OH 45402
(937) 224-5279; Fax (937) 224-5284
bha_dayton_admn@worldnet.att.net

3131 Executive Parkway, Suite 300
Toledo, OH 43606
(419) 535-3898; Fax (419) 531-4771
bhadet@coast.net

OKLAHOMA:

3030 NW Expressway, Suite 727
Oklahoma City, OK 73112
(405) 948-7668; Fax (405) 948-7869
bhaokc@telepath.com

7060 South Yale, Suite 707
Tulsa, OK 74136
(918) 491-9151; Fax (918) 491-9153
haldane@gorilla.net

OREGON:

1221 S.W. Yamhill, Suite 124
Portland, OR 97205
(503) 295-5926; Fax (503) 295-2639
bhacareers@aol.com

PENNSYLVANIA:

Parkview Tower
1150 First Avenue, Suite 385
King of Prussia, PA 19404 **(Philadelphia)**
(610) 491-9050; Fax (610) 491-9080
jobs@bhaldane.com

Three Gateway Center, 18 East
401 Liberty Avenue
Pittsburgh, PA 15222
(412) 263-5627; Fax (412) 263-2027
bhapittspa@aol.com

RHODE ISLAND:

1400 Bank Boston Plaza
Providence, RI 02903
(401) 461-9900; Fax (401) 461-0099
providence@haldane.com

SOUTH CAROLINA:

5000 Thurmond Mall, Suite 106
Columbia, SC 29201
(803) 799-9155; Fax (803) 799-9163
columbia@haldanestl.com

TENNESSEE:

7610 Gleason Drive, Suite 301
Knoxville, TN 37919
(423) 690-6767; Fax (423) 690-3990
bhaknox@worldnet.att.net

1661 International Drive, Suite 400
Memphis, TN 38120
(901) 820-4420; Fax (901) 818-3064
memphis@haldanestl.com

424 Church Street, Suite 1625
Nashville, TN 37219
(615) 742-8440; Fax (615) 742-8445
jobs@bhaldane.com

TEXAS:

Park Central VII, 12750 Merit Dr., Ste. 200
Dallas, TX 75251
(972) 503-4100; (Fax) 972-503-4445
bhadfw@ont.com

UTAH:

215 South State Street, Suite 200
Salt Lake City, UT 84111
(801) 355-4242; Fax (801) 355-3238
bhajobs@worldnet.att.net

VIRGINIA:

2101 Wilson Blvd., Suite 950
Arlington, VA 22201 **(DC)**
(703) 516-9122; Fax (703) 812-3001
jobs@bhaldane.com

6800 Paragon Place, Suite 106
Richmond, VA 23230
(804) 282-0470; Fax (804) 282-1983
jobs@bhaldane.com

WASHINGTON:

10900 N.E. 8th St., Suite 1122
Bellevue, WA 98004 **(Seattle)**
(425) 462-7308; Fax (425) 462-9670
careerspnw@aol.com

West 818 Riverside Drive, Suite 320
Spokane, WA 99201
(509) 325-7650; Fax (509) 325-7655
careersspo@aol.com

Tacoma Security Building
917 Pacific Avenue, Suite 400
Tacoma,WA 98402
(253) 383-8757; Fax (253) 383-0887
careersadv@aol.com

WISCONSIN:

4351 West College Ave., Suite 215
Appleton, WI 54914
(920) 831-7820; Fax (920) 831-7831
bhaappletn@aol.com

15800 W. Bluemound Road, Suite 320
Brookfield, WI 53005 **(Milwaukee)**
(414) 797-8055; Fax (414) 797-9002
bhamilw@aol.com

5315 Wall Street, Suite 220
Madison, WI 53718
(608) 246-2100; Fax (608) 246-2031
bhamadison@aol.com

Canada:

3027 Harvester Rd., Suite 105
Burlington, Ontario, Canada L7N 3G7
(905) 681-0180; Fax (905) 681-0181
haldane@bserv.com

One London Place,
255 Queens Avenue, Suite 2150
London, Ontario, Canada N6A 5R8
(519) 439-2580; Fax (519) 439-2587
bhaldane@ican.net

1250 Blvd. Rene-Levesque Ouest, Suite 2335
Montreal, Quebec, Canada H3B 4W8
(514) 938-0578; Fax (514) 938-9165
700617@ican.net

Manulife Place
55 Metcalfe Street, Suite 1460
Ottawa, Ontario, Canada K1P 6L5
(613) 234-2530; Fax (613) 234-2560
687131@ican.net

One Financial Place
One Adelaide Street East, Suite 2201
Toronto, Ontario, Canada M5C 2V9
(416) 363-9241; Fax (416) 363-9246
bhatoronto@aol.com

IBM Tower, Suite 1800
701 West Georgia Street
Vancouver, British Columbia V7Y 1C6
(604) 609-6661; Fax (604) 609-2638
bha@portal.ca

United Kingdom:

Cornwall Court
19 Cornwall Street
Birmingham 3 2DY UK
011-44-1212-243192; Fax 011-44-1212-005775
bhanorth@aol.com

2440 The Quadrant
Aztec West
Almondsbury, **Bristol** BS32 4AQ UK
011-44-1454-878506; Fax 011-44-1454-878606
temp@haldane.co.uk

Marcol House
289/293 Regent Street
London W1R 7PD UK
011-44-1712-909100; Fax 011-44-1712-909109
bha@haldane.co.uk

82 King Street
Manchester M2 4QW UK
011-44-1619-358070;
(Fax) 011-44-1619-358217
bhanorth@aol.com

Index